# Building a BeagleBone Black Super Cluster

Build and configure your own parallel computing
Beowulf cluster using BeagleBone Black ARM systems

**Andreas Josef Reichel**

BIRMINGHAM - MUMBAI

# Building a BeagleBone Black Super Cluster

First published: November 2014

Production reference: 1131114

Published by Packt Publishing Ltd.
Livery Place
35 Livery Street
Birmingham B3 2PB, UK.

ISBN 978-1-78398-944-7

www.packtpub.com

# Credits

**Author**

Andreas Josef Reichel

**Reviewers**

Georg Kaindl

Tor Oscar Olsson

Yogi A. Patel

Donald R. Poole, Jr.

**Commissioning Editor**

Amarabha Banerjee

**Acquisition Editor**

Owen Roberts

**Content Development Editor**

Anila Vincent

**Technical Editors**

Kunal Anil Gaikwad

Pramod Kumavat

**Copy Editor**

Stuti Srivastava

**Project Coordinator**

Neha Bhatnagar

**Proofreaders**

Simran Bhogal

Maria Gould

Ameesha Green

Paul Hindle

**Indexers**

Hemangini Bari

Mariammal Chettiyar

**Production Coordinator**

Nitesh Thakur

**Cover Work**

Nitesh Thakur

# About the Author

**Andreas Josef Reichel** was born in 1982 in Munich, Bavaria, to Josef and Ursula. He went to an elementary school from 1989 to 1993 and continued with lower secondary education for 4 years and started with middle school in 1996. In 1999, he finished school as the best graduate of the year. From 2000 to 2001, he went to Fachoberschule and got his subject-linked university entrance qualification, with which he began to study Physical Technology at the University of Applied Sciences in Munich. After two semesters, he got his preliminary diploma and began with general studies of Physics at the Ludwig Maximilian University of Munich in 2003. In 2011, he completed Dipl.-Phys. (Univ.) in experimental physics with the THz characterization of thin semiconductor films in photonics and optoelectronics. Now, he is working on his dissertation to Dr. rer. nat. on plasma etching processes for semiconductors at the Walter Schottky Institute of the Technische Universität München in Garching.

In his spare time, he has been learning programming languages such as BASIC, Pascal, C/C++, x86 and x64 Assembler, as well as HTML, PHP, JavaScript, and the database system MySQL and has been programming since he was 13 years old. Since 1995, he has been an active hobby musician in different accordion ensembles and orchestras. He also loves to learn about languages and drawing, and he began practicing Chinese martial arts in 2012. He invests most of his free time in hobby electronic projects and family genealogical research.

He was the co-author of *Charge carrier relaxation and effective masses in silicon probed by terahertz spectroscopy, S. G. Engelbrecht, A. J. Reichel, and R. Kersting, Journal of Applied Physics.*

I would like to thank my friends Bruno Lorenz and Stefan Mayr for all the great fun we had while programming. I'd also like to thank them for their help when I shared my hardware experiments with them; they were always open to discussions. I would like to dedicate this work to my daughter, Maria Sofie.

# About the Reviewers

**Georg Kaindl** is a hardware and software enthusiast with a diverse background in multiple fields, such as computer vision, compiler optimization, embedded systems programming, and real-time graphics. He earned an MSc degree at the Vienna University of Technology and has since been contracted for both Fortune 500 companies and start-ups. He has also established multiple software ventures himself. He also teaches courses on interaction design and advanced programming topics as an external lecturer at universities and other educational institutions. Apart from his professional work, he enjoys contributing to open source projects, such as the Arduino environment and the Linux kernel.

**Tor Oscar Olsson** was born in 1990 in Lund, Sweden. In 2009, he began studying Engineering and Computer Science at Lund University. Before and during his studies, he worked on several personal projects involving software development, configuration, and hardware.

During his last 2 years at Lund University, he worked in the Department of Computer Science at the Faculty of Engineering with different projects associated with robotics. Most of his time was spent developing and evaluating hard real-time communication protocols.

In 2014, he received his Master's degree after writing a thesis on solving linear systems efficiently; the thesis can be found at `http://www.lunduniversity.lu.se/o.o.i.s?id=24965&postid=4463318`.

**Yogi A. Patel** is a PhD student of Neuroengineering at the Georgia Institute of Technology, working on the design of neural interfaces, real-time systems, and electrical stimulation therapies. He has a background in computational science and biochemistry, with interests in entrepreneurship and academia. He teaches courses on bioelectricity and analog/digital circuit design, develops open source electrophysiology hardware (`www.puggleboard.com`) and software (`www.rtxi.org`), and contributes to the development of the Linux kernel.

**Donald R. Poole, Jr.** has a Bachelor of Science degree in Electrical Engineering and works at Southwest Research Institute (SwRI) as a research engineer, designing and developing wired and wireless communications, radars, and embedded systems for the U.S. government and industry. He has expertise in building custom embedded ARM Linux systems from the ground up for signal processing and robotics applications. He is currently part of a team of lead integrators and developers for the U.S. Army's Vehicular Integration for C4ISR/EW Interoperability (VICTORY) initiative for tactical vehicle and ground combat systems. He is happily married and has a young son, who he loves spending time with when he's not working. He enjoys playing his bass guitar and keyboard, apart from playing many sports.

# www.PacktPub.com

## Support files, eBooks, discount offers, and more

For support files and downloads related to your book, please visit www.PacktPub.com.

Did you know that Packt offers eBook versions of every book published, with PDF and ePub files available? You can upgrade to the eBook version at www.PacktPub.com and as a print book customer, you are entitled to a discount on the eBook copy. Get in touch with us at service@packtpub.com for more details.

At www.PacktPub.com, you can also read a collection of free technical articles, sign up for a range of free newsletters and receive exclusive discounts and offers on Packt books and eBooks.

http://PacktLib.PacktPub.com

Do you need instant solutions to your IT questions? PacktLib is Packt's online digital book library. Here, you can search, access, and read Packt's entire library of books.

## Why subscribe?

- Fully searchable across every book published by Packt
- Copy and paste, print, and bookmark content
- On demand and accessible via a web browser

## Free access for Packt account holders

If you have an account with Packt at www.PacktPub.com, you can use this to access PacktLib today and view 9 entirely free books. Simply use your login credentials for immediate access.

# Table of Contents

# Preface

In the beginning of the 20th century, a great mind began to think about his interests in technology and art. His name was Konrad Zuse. As a young man, he had been looking for fields where he could use his creativity, but he was somehow disappointed with fixed rules that gave him no space to apply any free thought. Having started with mechanical engineering, he soon switched over to architecture, where he was disappointed again because he could only draw predefined Doric and Ionic columns and could not create something he had in mind himself. So, he switched over to civil and construction engineering. During his studying years, he thought of automatization that could ease real-life tasks, such as automatically working cameras or programmable instruments that could simplify complicated and annoying calculation tasks. He also built the first working vending machine where one could select goods from a dial and retrieve them after inserting coins.

Konrad Zuse (1910-1995), the inventor of the freely programmable binary computer

Finally, he was possessed enough by the idea to invent a binary working computer, which he started to build in the living room of his parents' house, who were not quite amused about this. He was the first engineer who ever used the binary number system invented by Gottfried Wilhelm Leibniz (1646-1716). Based on this, he reinvented two-state logic without knowing that such a thing already existed. Using his ideas, he finally succeeded, after two years, in building the world's first working computer, the Z1, which he finished in 1937. It was a mechanical apparatus that used the motor of a vacuum cleaner, which seemed more practical to him compared to using electronic parts.

The Z1 was the first binary computer that had an input and output system, a memory, an arithmetical unit, and a program execution unit. Programs could be loaded from paper cards with hole patterns. However, the mechanical parts of the Z1 were not very reliable. Its successor, the Z2, worked with electronic relays and was able to perform floating point operations and possessed a 16-bit memory as well as a 10 Hz system clock.

At this time, computers were huge and filled whole rooms. However, development from electronic relays to electronic tubes soon increased the possible computation speed. The most famous computer that used such tubes was the Electronic Numerical Integrator and Computer (ENIAC). Its power supply had to provide almost 200 kW, which is 500 times more than what is required for standard computers nowadays. Addition or subtraction of a simple number took 200 microseconds, and calculating the root of a number took around a third of second.

Further developments in electronics and the amazing discovery of semiconductors laid down the fundament for the invention of the transistor. The first working bipolar transistor was invented at Bell Laboratories and was presented on December 23, 1947. It was for the first time that it was possible to control electronic currents with voltages in a much more reliable way.

In 1949, Werner Jacobi invented a semiconductor amplifier that used five transistors on one semiconductor substrate. This development was not noticed in the beginning, but it provided the basis for further miniaturization. This approach found more and more popularity from 1958 onward. Robert Noyce invented a fully integrated semiconductor circuit that also included its wire interconnections, which already used photo lithographic processes and diffusion processes for fabrication.

After several improvements in transistor fabrication, such as self-aligned gate structures, the semiconductor company Intel® developed the world's first universally functioning microprocessor for the Japanese calculator company Busicom. This led to the development of the first Central Processing Unit (CPU), which is the Intel 4004, and it was universally applicable. It was first made available on November 15, 1971.

The Intel 4004 microprocessor in a self-built vintage computer

The 4004 ran at a clock speed of maximum 740 kHz and consisted of around 2300 transistors. The execution of one command lasted eight cycles, which was one machine cycle. This led to a maximum throughput of 92500 instructions per second.

However, this was just the beginning. The number of bits the processors were able to work with at once was increased from four to eight, starting with the 8008 microprocessor. Also, speed and supported memory sizes increased dramatically over the first decade. Computers became affordable and are now an integral part of almost everybody's home.

Modern processors consist of billions of transistors and run at clock speeds of around 4 GHz, which leads to command throughputs of up to 4 billion instructions per second. Memory sizes increased from a few kilobytes to terabytes over the last decades and transistor sizes have shrunken by a factor of thousand from 10 microns to 15 nanometers.

Additionally, miniaturization has led to the possibility of building a fully working computer the size of a credit card with a million times more memory and 50,000 times less power consumption, which is a million times faster than ENIAC.

Combining several of these small computers can further increase their unimaginable calculation capacity, leading to the exciting world of parallel computations and super clusters.

In this book, you will learn about a state-of-the-art model of these very tiny computer boards, that is BeagleBone Black, which resembles a full computer system. Its abilities are far beyond what anybody could dream of 50 years ago. You will learn how to integrate several of these small boards into a fully working super computer cluster, giving you the possibility to freely scale up its calculation power.

Practical examples will demonstrate what this immense power is really useful for nowadays.

# What this book covers

*Chapter 1, BeagleBone Black System Board,* introduces you to the hardware and explains the handling and working principle of the BeagleBone Black system board. A very basic introduction to generic software programming is also provided.

*Chapter 2, Building a Beowulf Cluster,* shows you a step-by-step guide in order to build a super computer with only minimal hardware interconnecting several boards. The network interconnection and topology is explained in detail.

*Chapter 3, Operating System Setup and Configuration,* shows you exactly how to install the Ubuntu operating system used throughout this book. A step-by-step guide helps you configure the master and slave nodes, SSH, as well as basic developer tools. A simple method of data transfer between the cluster and an external computer is also shown.

*Chapter 4, Parallel Computing with OpenMPI and ScaLAPACK,* features the introduction and installation of the OpenMPI messaging system. This chapter provides the basis for scaling calculations of linear mathematical problems on the cluster nodes. This is shown with the popular library ScaLAPACK.

*Chapter 5, Advanced Solving of General Equation Systems,* enhances the previous chapter with advanced software libraries such as PETSc for linear and nonlinear problems as well as SLEPc for Eigenvalue problems. Example programs show you how to solve such equations on your cluster.

*Chapter 6, Scientific and Technological Examples of Parallel Computing,* shows you the final step in order to use deal.II, the highly sophisticated scientific finite element library for simulations and arbitrary dimensions. Example programs show you how to take your first steps in order to use this huge library to solve difficult equations with a state-of-the-art approach.

*Appendix, References,* gives a list of important links for various software and examples, which provide additional reference.

# What you need for this book

This book is based on the open source Linux operating system Ubuntu, which can easily be obtained and installed as described in the corresponding chapters. All configuration and further installation is based on open source standard software, which is under development and has long-term support. Links to the libraries are provided in the chapters and the appendix.

The mathematics and scientific libraries are downloaded from the Internet and are compiled on the BeagleBone Black system by the reader.

# Who this book is for

This book is intended for the interested reader, the part-time programmer, or the professional scientist. It is not necessary for the reader to know every detail of complex linear algebra or multidimensional finite element problems. It is also not necessary for the reader to be a professional software programmer. With a little interest and love for challenging software applications, everybody can use this book as a first step toward modern cluster computing as a hobby and for professional usage.

# Conventions

In this book, you will find a number of styles of text that distinguish between different kinds of information. Here are some examples of these styles, and an explanation of their meaning.

Code words in text, database table names, folder names, filenames, file extensions, pathnames, dummy URLs, user input, and Twitter handles are shown as follows: "The mmcblk0p1 and mmcblk0p2 partition, respectively, relate to the first and second partition of the first block device (the number zero), whereas the mmcblk1p1 and mmcblk1p2 partitions relate to the second block device (the number one)."

A block of code is set as follows:

```
int main() {

    return 0;
}
```

Any command-line input or output is written as follows:

```
mkdir ~/ubimage
sudo mount /dev/mmcblk0p2 ~/ubimage
```

**New terms** and **important words** are shown in bold. Words that you see on the screen, in menus or dialog boxes for example, appear in the text like this: "For this, go to the left-hand side window and open the **Add** menu with the green plus sign."

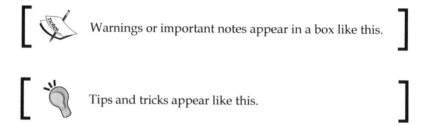

> Warnings or important notes appear in a box like this.

> Tips and tricks appear like this.

# Reader feedback

Feedback from our readers is always welcome. Let us know what you think about this book—what you liked or disliked. Reader feedback is important for us as it helps us develop titles that you will really get the most out of.

To send us general feedback, simply e-mail feedback@packtpub.com, and mention the book's title in the subject of your message.

If there is a topic that you have expertise in and you are interested in either writing or contributing to a book, see our author guide at www.packtpub.com/authors.

# Customer support

Now that you are the proud owner of a Packt book, we have a number of things to help you to get the most from your purchase.

# Downloading the example code

You can download the example code files from your account at http://www.packtpub.com for all the Packt Publishing books you have purchased. If you purchased this book elsewhere, you can visit http://www.packtpub.com/support and register to have the files e-mailed directly to you.

# Errata

Although we have taken every care to ensure the accuracy of our content, mistakes do happen. If you find a mistake in one of our books—maybe a mistake in the text or the code—we would be grateful if you could report this to us. By doing so, you can save other readers from frustration and help us improve subsequent versions of this book. If you find any errata, please report them by visiting http://www.packtpub.com/submit-errata, selecting your book, clicking on the **Errata Submission Form** link, and entering the details of your errata. Once your errata are verified, your submission will be accepted and the errata will be uploaded to our website or added to any list of existing errata under the Errata section of that title.

To view the previously submitted errata, go to https://www.packtpub.com/books/content/support and enter the name of the book in the search field. The required information will appear under the **Errata** section.

# Piracy

Piracy of copyrighted material on the Internet is an ongoing problem across all media. At Packt, we take the protection of our copyright and licenses very seriously. If you come across any illegal copies of our works in any form on the Internet, please provide us with the location address or website name immediately so that we can pursue a remedy.

Please contact us at copyright@packtpub.com with a link to the suspected pirated material.

We appreciate your help in protecting our authors and our ability to bring you valuable content.

# Questions

If you have a problem with any aspect of this book, you can contact us at questions@packtpub.com, and we will do our best to address the problem.

# 1
# BeagleBone Black System Board

While studying physics and natural science, I always felt that solving scientific or mathematical problems was the only way of really making use of a modern computer's speed and calculation power. Such problems appear in research, simulation, or visualization purposes, as well as in computer games. Playing around with computers and programming since the age of 13, I soon realized that linear problems such as equation systems can take a very long time to get solved on modern standard PCs, depending on the number of unknowns. Also, being interested in the miniaturization of hardware, I finally came across **BeagleBone Black (BBB)**, which is a credit-card-sized computer that can run Linux. I soon stumbled across some already realized supercomputer projects on the Web that utilize similar boards. Having read some articles about their scalability and capabilities, I decided to try and understand how to build and configure such a supercomputer with the more modern BBBs instead of Raspberry Pi. I succeeded in building my first self-built, low-cost supercomputer that is a **Beowulf** cluster, and now I will show you how to build your own. The common reason why people buy BBB is because of its fascinating hardware. There are a lot of other embedded systems such as Arduino Mega or Raspberry Pi, which were created in order to enable hobby programmers to start the development of their own hardware controls or other applications right away. Compared to Arduino Mega or other low-level products, BBB has 100 times or more computational power and a lot of other integrated features for the same price.

The technical specifications of BBB are introduced in this chapter. Alongside the basic hardware architecture and board features, you will get to know other useful information on the boot selection button and internal storage partitions. Coming to the operating system (OS) and software parts, the main focus will be on the OS used throughout this book and a basic understanding of programming languages and the development tools for later chapters.

The following topics will be covered:

- Explanation of the system board features
- Introduction to existing operating systems
- Understanding the partition structure with and without a microSD card
- Explanation of boot partition and boot failure recovery
- Introduction to the necessary programming environment for this book

The last point is especially written for hobbyists who might or might not have basic programming skills, as all the steps required to create your own software will be explained and kept at a basic level.

# Introducing the hardware

The BBB board is a complete, low-cost, energy-efficient, multipurpose development system with onboard Ethernet, flash storage, video controller, and much more. Its primary goal is to offer a true open hardware and community-supported embedded computer for developers and hobbyists. Compared to low-level embedded systems such as Arduino, BBB is a fully functional standalone PC that has the size of a credit card.

Without any expansion cards, the power required by a BBB is around 2.5 watts, which is 5 percent of the power required by a typical light bulb. Compared to a common Pentium III computer with the same clock frequency of 1 GHz, it only needs about 2.5 percent of its power requirement, and even has a better graphics card onboard, but has slightly less memory.

# The central processing unit

In general, the power of a computer is defined by the speed of its components. Most critical are the main memory, its bus interconnection, and the central processing unit (CPU). The slowest interconnecting path between faster components is called the *bottleneck* and defines the overall system's performance. On modern CPUs, the memory interface is on-die, which means that it is integrated into the silicon chip. This offers maximum performance and avoids any bottlenecks between the CPU and the main memory. This is also the case with BBB.

BBB's heart is the Sitara ™ ARM ® Cortex-A8 32-bit processor from Texas Instruments with a programmable clock driven at 1 GHz by factory settings. Interestingly, on some of my boards, the XAM3359AZCZ100 version of the CPU is used, which has a maximum frequency of 800 MHz according to TI. Despite this, it is driven at 1000 MHz on BBB without any problems. According to the manual, it was changed to XAM3358 in the board revision C. The architecture is RISC, which means that the CPU only needs one clock cycle to execute a command. This makes the Cortex-A8 faster than a typical Intel P3 with the same clock frequency if one focuses on standard instructions. Also, the CPU supports the NEON instruction set, which gives BBB a great advantage over Raspberry Pi.

Under full processor utilization, the board gets quite warm. This is not a problem if it is used as a standalone board. However, if there is more than one board in a small area or even if the boards are stacked on top of each other, they will need some cooling in order to avoid overheating. An example of a cheap cooling system is given in *Chapter 2, Building a Beowulf Cluster*.

The figure in the next section shows us the internal CPU architecture that also provides very sophisticated features such as a touchscreen controller and a 3D graphics acceleration on-die.

# I/O interfaces and control buttons

The actual purpose of BBB was to provide a development platform that is easy to program and can be used to control or regulate other hardware. In other words, it must be able to measure and output signals that are easy to interface in the hardware and software. To provide this capability, two 46-pin headers are available for **general-purpose I/O (GPIO)**. These pins use a 3.3 volt logic for I/O. A higher voltage level might result in damaging the CPU. The board also provides two **programmable real-time units (PRUs)** for time-critical applications. Please refer to the hardware manual for a detailed description. In this book, no I/O operation is described, as they are not used in the BBB cluster.

Besides general-purpose I/O, the board also provides the following:

- A RJ45 network jack
- A 5V power jack
- A USB client
- A USB host port
- A HDMI jack for video and audio support
- A serial port header that is useable for debugging

The system can be powered by either the 5V power jack or the USB client port using the preinstalled operating system. However, using the operating system as described in this book, we can see that only the 5V power jack will work. This means that the boards in the final cluster configuration cannot be powered up using a USB power supply. Please refer to *Chapter 2, Building a Beowulf Cluster*, for information on how to build a cheap and efficient power supply. This book only describes the usage of the RJ45 network interface for installation, configuration, and user control via SSH. Thus, it is not necessary to make use of the HDMI port in cluster applications. The onboard network controller works with 10/100 megabit/s.

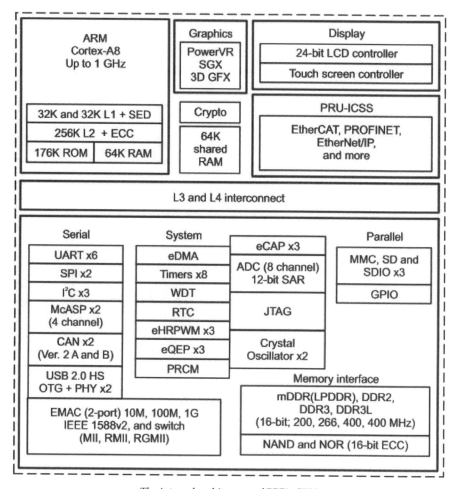

The internal architecture of BBB's CPU

The following image and list gives you an overview of the important onboard ports, plugs, and control buttons; **a** indicates a 5V power jack, **b** indicates an RJ45 Ethernet port, **c** indicates a general-purpose I/O with serial header on its right, **d** indicates a USB host port, **e** indicates status LEDs, **f** indicates the reset button, **g** indicates the power button, **h** indicates the CPU, **i** indicates the boot-selection button, **j** indicates a USB client port, **k** indicates the microSD slot, and **l** indicates the mini HDMI port:

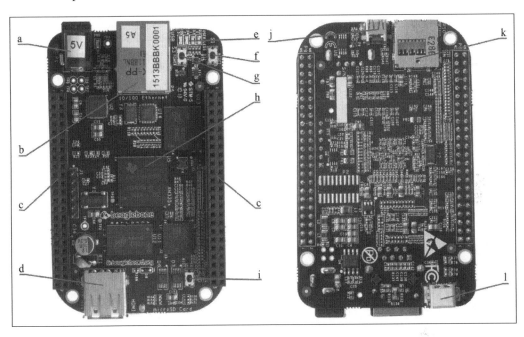

While the power and reset buttons are used in the same manner as they are used on PCs, the boot-selection button is used to select the boot sector located in either the internal ROM or on the external microSD card. This function is very useful in order to recover a misconfigured or non-bootable system.

# The onboard memory and flash storage

BBB is equipped with 512 MB of DDR3 RAM, which possesses a higher bandwidth compared to the competitor, which is Raspberry Pi, which uses DDR2 RAM. It is not possible to extend the physical RAM on a single BBB; however, this is not important when performing cloud computing because this makes use of distributed memory.

For nonvolatile storage, 2 or 4 GB of 8-bit eMMC flash memory—depending on your board revision—is available onboard. This is enough to install all the required software along with the operating system in order to perform the highly sophisticated computations described in this book. Any dynamic libraries will be installed in a common network shared folder. The storage capacity can also be extended using the free microSD card slot that provides more virtual memory or additional storage capacity. You should refer to the documentation of your specific board version to see supported microSD card sizes. In this book, an additional card with 16 GB size will be used for the master-node board, which will be explained in *Chapter 3, Operating System Setup and Configuration*.

# The storage memory partition structure

Let's first explain what partitions are and why they are used. Partitions are logical divisions of storage space divided into multiple logical units, providing a convenient way of storage management. Each partition can have its own filesystem, and thus, it can be formatted separately. Also, for virtual memory a specific type of partition, a so-called swap partition can be used. Every block device, which means every memory device with random access and consisting of discrete blocks such as sectors, can be partitioned.

Each operating system usually has a boot partition where important system files that are in charge of starting up the system are stored. A system can have more than one operating system where a boot menu can provide the possibility of selecting a specific boot partition on each system startup.

It is very important to understand the partition structure of the BBB storage memory in order to know how to install alternative operating systems. By default, there is no extension microSD card installed, and the internal flash memory is divided into two partitions. If you boot up the preinstalled operating system from the internal memory, there will be two partitions for the internal and two partitions for the optional uninstalled microSD card. Furthermore, there will be two virtual partitions that represent the boot loader for the internal and external memory. The latter two are permanent and cannot be accidentally overwritten. The kernel of the preinstalled Linux version, like any other version, will map the storage partitions in its local filesystem to the /dev directory.

The following table shows the existing partitions if they are booted from the internal flash memory:

| Partition | Location |
| --- | --- |
| /dev/mmcblk0p1 | The first block device and the first partition |
| /dev/mmcblk0p2 | The first block device and the second partition |
| /dev/mmcblk1p1 | The second block device and the first partition |
| /dev/mmcblk1p2 | The second block device and second partition |
| /dev/mmcblk0boot0 | The boot code partition 1 |
| /dev/mmcblk0boot1 | The boot code partition 2 |

The mmcblk0p1 and mmcblk0p2 partitions, respectively, relate to the first and second partitions of the first block device (the number zero), whereas the mmcblk1p1 and mmcblk1p2 partitions relate to the second block device (the number one).The order of the block devices changes if an external microSD card is installed and booted.

 If there is no external microSD card installed, the internal memory is /dev/mmcblk0; if it is installed, the internal memory is /dev/mmcblk1 instead.

# The boot-selection button

The boot-selection button enables the user to select the boot code. If it is pressed during the system startup, the mmcblkXboot1 partition is selected, which will boot up the first partition of the microSD card. If it is not pressed, the system will load the internal boot partition code using mmcblkXboot0. The letter x means that boot1 and boot0 can be mapped onto either the first or second block device, which is irrelevant. The preinstalled boot sector will try to load the operating system on any inserted microSD card on its own. This will only work if the kernel located there is compatible. If it is not, the system will not boot up and will hang. This means that if you insert a microSD card with an alternative operating system for the first time, you have to push the boot-selection button until you see the system starting up (indicated by the status LEDs flickering). This only works if you cycle the board power, which means that you need a cold start and should not use the reset button.

This will be explained in *Chapter 3, Operating System Setup and Configuration*, which talks about how to install another Linux operating system and work with system partitions and filesystems in detail.

# Recovering a boot failure

Whenever you encounter a boot problem and cannot start up your BBB with the operating system on the internal eMMC flash, you can use a failsafe microSD card that you set up earlier in order to boot up the system. For this purpose, you just have to insert the microSD card into the slot and push the boot-selection button before you power on the system and hold it until it boots. It is always a good idea to keep a working system image on a microSD card for such purposes.

# Operating systems

BBB up to version A5C and built before May 2014 comes with a preinstalled operating system, namely the **Angstrom** Linux distribution. Later versions come with the Debian Linux distribution. Texas Instruments provides two releases: an Android and a Linux operating system. All the examples in this book are based on the Ubuntu Linux distribution; however, it is a question of personal taste which Linux distribution you want to use. If you decide to use another distribution, you might have to figure out how to compile your software and install the required packages on your own. There is, however, a chance that packages used throughout this book for Ubuntu might also work with other Linux distributions. Android does not support general Linux software and cannot be used to build a cluster with the means described in this book.

# ARMhf images

Linux operating systems are available for a vast variety of different computer platforms such as PowerPC, x86, IA-64, ARM, and many more. An interesting feature of the CPU used on BBBs is the implementation of floating point instructions. This means that mathematical operations based on non-integer values can be executed by hardware rather than software, and thus they are carried out much faster. **ARMhf** stands for **ARM hard float** architecture. To make use of this advantage, a special operating system image is used throughout this book, namely the Ubuntu-12.04-armhf image from John Clark.

# The Ubuntu 12.04 ARMhf Linux system

The Ubuntu 12.04 Linux distribution, compiled for the ARMhf platform, can be obtained from the home page of John Clark's website at `http://www.armhf.com/download/`. Please keep in mind that Linux systems and software are updated a lot. If you are not able to get exactly the same software as that used in this book, you can try a newer one or download the version from the download section accompanying this book. You will find more details on how to download and install the operating system in *Chapter 2, Building a Beowulf Cluster*.

> **Downloading the example code**
>
> You can download the example code files from your account at `http://www.packtpub.com` for all the Packt Publishing books you have purchased. If you purchased this book elsewhere, you can visit `http://www.packtpub.com/support` and register to have the files e-mailed directly to you.

# Software programming

The most important part of a good computer is good software. Without good software, specifically optimized for its hardware, the full computational power cannot be utilized. In this book, I will show you how to build a supercomputer cluster that gains its high-speed computational power from distributing certain tasks to other its via networking. For this purpose, special software is required and has to be compiled from the source code. How this works and what nodes are will be explained in *Chapter 2, Building a Beowulf Cluster*, and *Chapter 3, Operating System Setup and Configuration*.

# The open source philosophy

Although there are a lot of already existing helpful software packages, it is very important to understand that Linux is an open source operating system written for an open source community. Usually, Windows users are frustrated when they gain first contact with open source software, because they are used to having already working and easy-to-install software. A huge disadvantage is that these software packets are compiled for a standard platform and might not be optimized to a specific computer that they are installed on. Another problem is that if software components of the operating system are updated but older versions are required by the user software, instabilities might arise or completely different interfaces might disrupt the software functionality completely.

# Software modularity and dependencies

Linux is a highly modular operating system. The whole system is built on the philosophy of open software, which means that every part of the operating system can be compiled from available open source code. This source code is then compiled by standard programming languages such as C, C++, FORTRAN, Assembler, and others in order to build binary code specifically optimized for certain hardware. The technique by which software is built does not differ much from Windows or Linux operating systems. For the beginner, it might be hard to produce a working compiled program starting from source code because usually, there are a lot of software dependencies such as missing software libraries or other programs that code is based upon. In this case, it might be hard to find all the required libraries, especially when newer versions that have changed in interfaces such as function definitions are available. On the other hand, a dependency can soon lead to several others so that the search for all the required libraries grows exponentially and takes a lot of time.

Also, on certain hardware, some well-established compiling parameters do not work and have to be modified or bug fixes have to be found. This can make the simple task of "just compiling software" an unsolvable problem for beginners. Thanks to the rising community of hobby programmers and Linux enthusiasts, there are a lot of forums online that can be searched for such problems. Often, solutions are present, and if not, there can be hints that point us in the right direction, at least.

The following sections will explain the basics of creating software on Linux operating systems with standard programming environments. It is written for hobby enthusiasts who might or might not have already tried and programmed their own software. Although existing knowledge is very helpful, it is not required in order to understand the following explanations.

# The source code and programming languages

Each computer program consists of binary code, which means a sequence of two states usually described as zero and one. A specific state is called a **bit**. Four of these bits make up a so-called **nibble** and eight make up a **byte**. Several bytes can be described as a **word**, a **double word**, or a **quad word**. The following table gives you a small summary of the most important data sizes:

| Amount of bits | Amount of bytes | Special name |
| --- | --- | --- |
| 4 | 1/2 | nibble |
| 8 | 1 | byte |
| 16 | 2 | word |
| 32 | 4 | double word |
| 64 | 8 | quad word |

A central processor does nothing else except interpreting bit sequences as commands. These commands are called instructions and tell the CPU what to do. This is the lowest level of programming, which is the so-called machine language. Machine language is, except to certain freaky people, not human-readable. For example, it is not obvious that the binary code 1011 0100 0100 1100 1100 1101 0010 0001 is the end of an MS-DOS program.

# Low-level programming

Low-level programming means the direct programming of machine language. Of course, this has to happen in a human-readable way. One possibility to simplify 1011 0100 0100 1100 is given by using another number system, such as the hexadecimal system, resulting in 0xB4 0x4C. This is better, but it's still not readable by humans. The final simplification is the invention of so-called mnemonics. For example, on Intel x86-platforms, 0xB4 0x4C would mean mov ah, 0x4C in this mnemonics language. Now, one can understand that this code sets the CPU register named ah to the value of 0x4C. This language as well as the software that translates this back into bits is called Assembler.

Assembler has its advantages and disadvantages. One big advantage is that the resulting software does exactly what you programmed. This means that there is no optimization that modifies your code and you can program very effectively in size and speed. One big disadvantage, however, is the problem that each CPU has its own instruction set. This means that our Sitara CPU will not understand the preceding example, because it has no ah register. For any real problems we want to solve using computers, we are primarily interested in the nature of the problem and not the nature of the CPU used in the computer. To make programming independent of the used computer platform, there exist so-called high-level programming languages.

# High-level programming

High-level programming languages consist of keywords, syntax, and grammar, as with every spoken language. The keywords define the vocabulary that can be used, whereas syntax and grammar define the exact utilization and order of these keywords. To understand this, we should have a look at how a simple loop will look in a low-level language compared to a high-level language.

The following example shows us that a simple loop already needs four different instructions in Assembler, while it can be realized by a relatively simple `for` keyword in the high-level language C++:

| Low level (Assembler) | High level (C++) |
|---|---|
| mov cx, 0 | for (int j = 0; j < 345; j++) { |
| @mark1: | other code... |
|    other code.. | } |
| inc cx | |
| cmp cx, 345 | |
| jne @mark1 | |

A low-level language compared to a high-level language

While C++ is a general-purpose high-level programming language, there are also languages that are more specifically optimized. One example is FORTRAN, which is mainly used for mathematical problems due to its ability to define matrices and other mathematical structures very easily.

# The compiler toolchain

Once the required code has been written and is ready to be translated from its human-readable form into machine language, there is a certain sequence of tools that have to be used. This toolset is called the compiler toolchain:

1. Firstly, the code is treated by the **compiler** itself. The compiler translates the high-level language to a low-level language, mostly Assembler.

2. It is then translated to **object** files. Usually, these two processes are performed by only one compiler internally.

3. The object files then have the binary format and can be executed theoretically. However, the OS must know a few things in order to execute programs correctly. It must be told where in the main memory the program has to be loaded, how much memory it uses, which libraries it needs, and so on. To fulfill these requirements, we need to link the program.

4. The so-called linker combines one or more object files and adds information that's specific to the OS in use.

5. The final program then consists of a special **executable format** generated by the linker and incorporating the object files produced by the compiler. In Linux, this executable format is called **Executable and Linking Format (ELF)**.

The whole process is depicted in the following diagram:

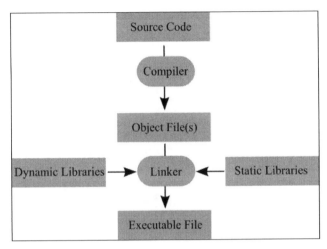

Software compilation and simple toolchain

Another important feature of the linker is its capability to embed the required libraries into the executable file. This is called **static linking**. The program can then be used on other computers that do not have that specific library installed. The opposite of static linking is **dynamic linking**. In this case, only a stub of the library is linked into the program that tells the OS which library to provide. Dynamically-linked programs are smaller in size but always need their libraries.

In all examples, the main focus will be on C++. Some of the modules are only available as FORTRAN code; however, once compiled, their functions can also be accessed from C++ programs.

# Summary

In this chapter, BeagleBone Black was introduced, starting with its hardware and key features. It was compared with other platforms regarding its power and energy requirements. Special attention was paid to the internal architecture of the central processing unit, the I/O-interfaces, and control buttons, as well as the embedded memory features.

For the following system setup, the internal flash partition system was described and special caution was taken on the variable partition mapping regarding an optional microSD card expansion.

The default boot mechanism and how it can be altered using the onboard boot selection button was explained. It was also mentioned how to unbrick the system if it fails to boot.

A short description of available operating systems was given as well as an explanation of the importance of native floating point support. The chapter ended with a short introduction to the basics of software programming, keeping an eye on the basic functionality of compilers and linkers. The difference between static and dynamic linking was explained, which will be of further importance in the next chapter. Missing elements such as data types will be explained where necessary.

In the next chapter, we will cover practical things. I will show you how to connect the boards, build a simple frame, and how to get a cheap power supply. You will also be introduced to the basic network structure and the general idea of a Beowulf cluster's topology.

# 2
# Building a Beowulf Cluster

A Beowulf cluster is nothing more than a bunch of computers interconnected by Ethernet and running with a Linux or BSD operating system. A key feature is the communication over IP (Internet Protocol) that distributes problems among the boards. The entity of the boards or computers is called a cluster and each board or computer is called a node.

In this chapter, we will first see what is really required for each board to run inside a cluster environment. You will see examples of how to build a cheap and scalable cluster housing and how to modify an ATX power supply in order to use it as a power source. I will then explain the network interconnection of the Beowulf cluster and have a look at its network topology. The chapter concludes with an introduction to the microSD card usage for installation images and additional swap space as well as external network storage.

The following topics will be covered:

- Describing the minimally required equipment
- Building a scalable housing
- Modifying an ATX power source
- Introducing the Beowulf network topology
- Managing microSD cards
- Using external network storage

We will first start with a closer look at the utilization of a single BBB and explain the minimal hardware configuration required.

# Minimal configuration and optional equipment

BBB is a single-board computer that has all the components needed to run Linux distributions that support ARMhf platforms. Due to the very powerful network utilities that come with Linux operating systems, it is not necessary to install a mouse or keyboard. Even a monitor is not required in order to install and configure a new BBB. First, we will have a look at the minimal configuration required to use a single board over a network.

## Minimal configuration

A very powerful interface of Linux operating systems is its standard support for SSH. SSH is the abbreviation of Secure Shell, and it enables users to establish an authenticated and encrypted network connection to a remote PC that provides a Shell. Its command line can then be utilized to make use of the PC without any local monitor or keyboard. SSH is the secure replacement for the telnet service. The following diagram shows you the typical configuration of a local area network using SSH for the remote control of a BBB board:

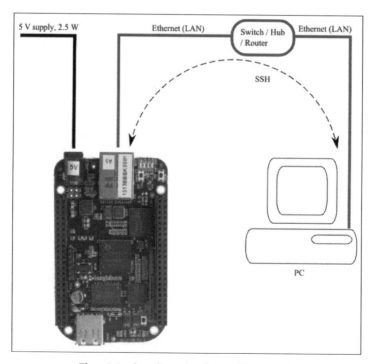

The minimal configuration for the SSH control

SSH is a key feature of Linux and comes preinstalled on most distributions. If you use Microsoft ® Windows™ as your host operating system, you will require additional software such as putty, which is an SSH client that is available at `http://www.putty.org`. On Linux and Mac OS, there is usually an SSH client already installed, which can be started using the `ssh` command.

## Using a USB keyboard

It is practical for several boards to be configured using the same network computer and an SSH client. However, if a system does not boot up, it can be hard for a beginner to figure out the reason. If you get stuck with such a problem and don't find a solution using SSH, or the SSH login is not possible for some reason anymore, it might be helpful to use a local keyboard and a local monitor to control the problematic board such as a usual PC. Installing a keyboard is possible with the onboard USB host port. A very practical way is to use a wireless keyboard and mouse combination. In this case, you only need to plug the wireless control adapter into the USB host port.

## Using the HDMI adapter and monitor

Using the BBB board supports high definition graphics and, therefore, uses a mini HDMI port for the video output. In order to use a monitor, you need an adapter for mini HDMI to HDMI, DVI, or VGA, respectively.

## Building a scalable board-mounting system

The following image shows you the finished board housing with its key components as well as some installed BBBs. Here, **a** indicates the threaded rod with the straw as the spacer, **b** indicates BeagleBone Black, **c** indicates the Ethernet cable, **d** indicates 3.5" hard disc cooling fans, **e** indicates the 5 V power cable, and **f** indicates the plate with drilled holes.

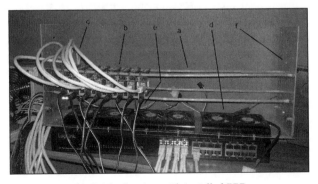

The finished casing with installed BBBs

One of the most important things that you have to consider before building a super computer is the space you require. It is not only important to provide stable and practical housing for some BBB boards, but also to keep in mind that you might want to upgrade the system to more boards in the future. This means that you require a scalable system that is easy to upgrade. Also, you need to keep in mind that every single board requires its own power and has to be accessible by hand (reset, boot-selection, and the power button as well as the memory card, and so on). The networking cables also need some place depending on their lengths. There are also flat Ethernet cables that need less space. The tidier the system is built, the easier it will be to track down errors or exchange faulty boards, cables, or memory cards.

However, there is a more important point. Although the BBB boards are very power-efficient, they get quite warm depending on their utilization. If you have 20 boards stacked onto each other and do not provide sufficient space for air flow, your system will overheat and suffer from data loss or malfunctions.

Insufficient air flow can result in the burning of devices and other permanent hardware damage. Please remember that I'm not liable for any damages resulting from an insufficient cooling system.

Depending on your taste, you can spend a lot of money on your server housing and put some lights inside and make it glow like a Christmas tree. In this book, however, I will show you very cheap housing, which is easy and fast to build and still robust enough, scalable, and practical to use.

# Board-holding rods

The key idea of my board installation is to use the existing corner holes of the BBB boards and attach the boards on four rods in order to build a horizontal stack. This stack is then held by two side plates and a base plate. Usually, when I experiment and want to build a prototype, it is helpful not to predefine every single measurement, and then invest money into the sawing and cutting of these parts. Instead, I look around in some hobby markets and see what they have and think about whether I can use these parts. However, drilling some holes is not unavoidable. When you get to drilling holes and using screws and threads, you might know or not know that there are two different systems. One is the metric system and the other is the English system. The BBB board has four holes and their size fits to 1/8" in the English or M3 in the metric system. According to the international standard, this book will only name metric dimensions.

For easy and quick installation of the boards, I used four M3 threaded rods that are obtainable at model making or hobby shops. I got mine at Conrad Electronic. For the base plates, I went to a local raw material store. The following diagram shows you the mounting hole positions for the side walls with the dimensions of BBB (dashed line). The measurements are given for the English and metric system.

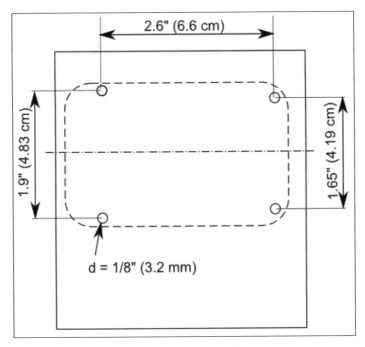

The mounting hole's positions

# Board spacers

As mentioned earlier, it is important to leave enough space between the boards in order to provide finger access to the buttons and, of course, for airflow. First, I mounted each board with eight nuts. However, when you have 16 boards installed and want to uninstall the eighth board from the left, then it will take you a lot of time and nerves to get the nuts along the threaded rods. A simple solution with enough stability is to use short parts of straws. You can buy some thick drinking straws and cut them into equally long parts, each of two or three centimeters in length. Then, you can put them between the boards onto the threaded rods in order to use them as spacers. Of course, this is not the most stable way, but it is sufficient, cheap, and widely available.

# Cooling system

One nice possibility I found for cooling the system is to use hard disk fans. They are not so cheap but I had some lying around for years. Usually, they are mounted to the lower side of 3.5" hard discs, and their width is approximately the length of one BBB. So, they are suitable for the base plate of our casing and can provide enough air flow to cool the whole system. I installed two with two fans each for eight boards and a third one for future upgrades. The following image shows you my system with eight boards installed:

A board housing with BBBs and cooling system

Once you have built the housing with a cooling system, you can install your boards. The next step will be the connection of each board to a power source as well as the network interconnection. Both are described in the following sections.

# Using a low-cost power source

I have seen a picture on the Web where somebody powered a dozen older Beagle Boards with a lot of single DC adapters and built everything into a portable case. The result was a huge mess of cables. You should always try to keep your cables well organized in order to save space and improve the cooling performance. Using an ATX power supply with a cable tree can save you a lot of money compared to buying several standalone power supplies. They are stable and can also provide some protection for hardware, which cheap DC adapters don't always do. In the following section, I will explain the power requirements and how to modify an ATX power supply to fit our needs.

# Power requirements

If you do not use an additional keyboard and mouse and only onboard flash memory, one board needs around 500 mA at 5 V voltage, which gives you a total power of 2.5 Watts for one board. Depending on the installed memory card or other additional hardware, you might need more.

 Please note that using the Linux distribution described in this book is not compatible with the USB-client port power supply. You have to use the 5 V power jack. Please refer to *Chapter 1, BeagleBone Black System Board*.

# Power cables

If you want to use an ATX power supply, then you need to build an adapter from the standard PATA or SATA power plugs to a low voltage plug that fits the 5 V jack of the board. You need a 5.5/2.1 mm low voltage plug and they are obtainable from VOLTCRAFT with cables already attached. I got mine from Conrad Electronics (item number 710344). Once you have got your power cables, you can build a small distribution box.

# Modifying the ATX power supply

ATX power supplies are widely available and power-efficient. They cost around 60 dollars, providing more than 500 Watts of output power. For our purpose, we will only need most power on the 5 V rail and some for fans on the 12 V rail. It is not difficult to modify an ATX supply. The trick is to provide the soft-on signal, because ATX supplies are turned on from the mainboard via a soft-on signal on the green wire. If this green wire is connected to the ground, it turns on. If the connection is lost, it turns off. The following image shows you which wires of the ATX mainboard plug have to be cut and attached to a manual switch in order to build a manual on/off switch:

The ATX power plug with a green and black wire, as indicated by the red circle, cut and soldered to a switch

As we are using the 5 V and most probably the 12 V rail (for the cooling fans) of the power supply, it is not necessary to add resistors. If the output voltage of the supply is far too low, this means that not enough current is flowing for its internal regulation circuitry. If this happens, you can just add a 1/4 Watt 200 Ohms resistor between any +5 V (red) and GND (neighboring black) pin to drain a current of 25 mA. This should never happen when driving the BBB boards, as their power requirements are much higher and the supply should regulate well.

The following image shows you the power cable distribution box. I soldered the power cables together with the cut ends of a PATA connector to a PCB board.

The power cable distribution box

What could happen is that the resistance of one PATA wire is too high and the voltage drop leads to a supply voltage of below 4.5 Volts. If that happens, some of the BBB boards will not power up. Either you need to retry booting these boards separately by their power button later when all others are booted up, or you need to use two PATA wires instead of one to decrease the resistance. Please have a look if this is possible with your power supply and if the two 5 V lines you want to connect do not belong to different regulation circuitries.

# Setting up the network backbone

To interconnect BBB boards via Ethernet, we need a switch or a hub. There is a difference in the functionality between a switch and a hub:

- With hubs, computers can communicate with each other. Every computer is connected to the hub with a separate Ethernet cable. The hub is nothing more than a multiport repeater. This means that it just repeats all the information it receives for all other ports, and every connected PC has to decide whether the data is for it or not. This produces a lot of network traffic and can slow down the speed.

- Switches in comparison can control the flow of network traffic based on the address information in each packet. It learns which traffic packets are received by which PC and then forwards them only to the proper port. This allows simultaneous communication across the switch and improves the bandwidth. This is the reason why switches are the preferred choice of network interconnection for our BBB Beowork cluster.

The following table summarizes the main differences between a hub and a switch:

|  | Hub | Switch |
|---|---|---|
| **Traffic control** | no | yes |
| **Bandwidth** | low | high |

I bought a 24-port Ethernet switch on eBay with 100 Megabit/s ports. This is enough for the BBB boards. The total bandwidth of the switch is 2.4 Gigabit/s.

# The network topology

The typical network topology is a star configuration. This means that every BBB board has its own connection to the switch, and the switch itself is connected to the local area network (LAN). On most Beowulf clusters, there is one special board called the master node. This master node is used to provide the bridge between the cluster and the rest of the LAN. All users (if there are more persons that use the cluster) log in to the master node, and it is only responsible for user management and starting the correct programs on specified nodes. It usually doesn't contribute to any calculation tasks.

However, as BBB only has one network connector, it is not possible to use it as a bridge, because a bridge requires two network ports:

- One connected to the LAN.
- The other connected to the switch of the cluster.

Because of this, we only define one node as the master node, providing some special software features but also contributing to the calculations of the cluster. This way, all BBBs contribute to the overall calculation power, and we do not need any special hardware to build a network bridge.

Regarding security, we can manage everything with SSH login rules and the kernel firewall, if required. The following diagram shows you the network topology used in this book. Every BBB has its own IP address, and you have to reserve the required amount of IP addresses in your LAN. They do not have to be successive; however, it makes it easier if you note down every IP for every board. You can give the boards hostnames such as node1, node2, node3, and so on to make them easier to follow. You'll be shown how to do this in *Chapter 3, Operating System Setup and Configuration*.

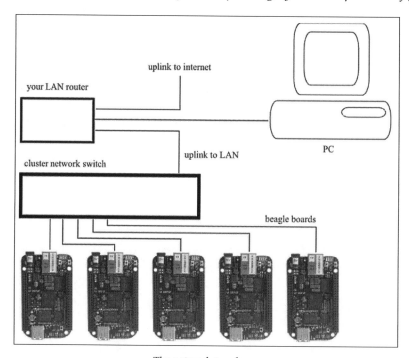

The network topology

# The RJ45 network cables

There is only one thing you have to keep in mind regarding RJ45 Ethernet cables and 100 Megabit/s transmission speed. There are crossover cables and normal ones. The crossover cables have crossed lines regarding data transmission and receiving. This means that one cable can be used to connect two PCs without a hub or switch. Most modern switches can detect when data packets collide, which means when they are received on the transmitting ports and then automatically switch over the lines again. This feature is called auto MDI-X or auto-uplink. If you have a newer switch, you don't need to pay attention to which sort of cable you buy. Usually, normal RJ45 cables without crossover are the preferred choice.

# The Ethernet multiport switch

As described earlier, we use an Ethernet switch rather than a hub. When buying a switch, you have to decide how many ports you want. For future upgrades, you can also buy an 8-port switch, for example, and later, if you want to go from seven boards (one port for the uplink) to 14 boards, you can upgrade with a second 8-port switch and connect both to the LAN. If you want to build a big system from the beginning, you might want to buy a 24-port switch or an even bigger one. The following image shows you my 24-port Ethernet switch with some connected RJ45 cables below the board housing:

A 24-port cluster switch

# The storage memory

One thing you might want to think of in the beginning is the amount of space you require for applications and data. The standard version of BBB has 2 GB flash memory onboard and newer ones have 4 GB. In this book, I describe my strategy of using one additional memory card for the master node and additional external network storage for shared libraries.

A critical feature of computational nodes is the amount of RAM they have installed. On BBB, this is only 512 MB. If you are of the opinion that this is not enough for your tasks, then you can extend the RAM by installing Linux on an external SD card and create a swap partition on it. However, you have to keep in mind that the external swap space is much slower than the DDR3 memory (MB/s compared to GB/s). If the software is nicely programmed, data can always be sufficiently distributed on the nodes, and each node does not need much RAM. However, with more complicated libraries and tasks, you might want to upgrade some day. In this book, we only expand the virtual memory of the master node with the swap space on the microSD card.

# Installing images on microSD cards

For the installation of Linux, we will need Linux Root File System Images on the microSD card. It is always a good idea to keep these cards for future repair or extension purposes. I keep one installation SD for the master node and one for all slave nodes. When I upgrade the system to more slave nodes, I can just insert the installation SD and easily incorporate the new system with a few commands.

# The swap space on an SD card

Usually, it should be possible to boot Linux from the internal memory and utilize the external microSD card solely as the swap space. However, I had problems utilizing the additional space as it was not properly recognized by the system. I obtained best results when booting from the same card I want the swap partition on. How exactly this works will be described in *Chapter 3, Operating System Setup and Configuration*.

# The external network storage

To reduce the size of the used software, it is always a good idea to compile it dynamically. Each node you want to use for computations has to start the same program. Programs have to be accessible by each node, which means that you would have to install every program on every node. This is a lot of work when adding additional boards and is a waste of memory in general.

To circumvent this problem, I use external network storage on the basis of Samba. The master node can then access the Samba share and create a share for all the client nodes by itself. This way, each node has access to the same software and data, and upgrades can be performed easily. Also, the need for local storage memory is reduced. Important libraries that have to be present on each local filesystem can be introduced by hard links pointing to the network storage location. The following image shows you the storage system of my BBB cluster:

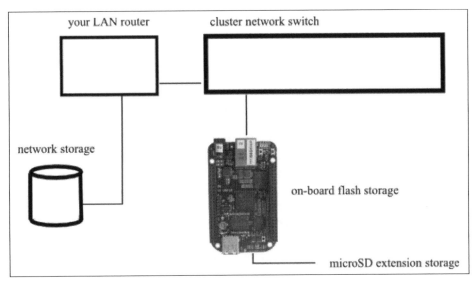

The storage topology

Some of you might worry when I chose Samba over NFS and think that a 100 Megabit networking is too slow for cluster computations. First of all, I chose Samba because I was used to it and it is well known to most hobbyists. It is very easy to install, and I have used it for over 10 years. Only thing you have to keep in mind is that using Samba will cause your filesystem to treat capital and small letters equally. So, your Linux filenames (ext2, ext3, ext4, and so on) will behave like FAT/NTFS filenames.

Regarding the network bandwidth, a double value will require 8 bytes of memory and thus, you can transfer a maximum of 2.4 billion double values per second on a hub with 24 ports and 100 Megabit/s. Additionally, libraries are optimized to keep the network talk as low as possible and solve as much as possible on the local CPU memory system. Thus, for most applications, the construction as described earlier will be sufficient.

# Summary

In this chapter, you were introduced to the whole cluster concept regarding its hardware and interconnection. You were shown a working system configuration using only the minimally required amount of equipment and also some optional possibilities. A description of very basic housing including a cooling system was given as an example for a cheap yet nicely scalable possibility to mount the boards. You also learned how to build a cost-efficient power supply using a widely available ATX supply, and you were shown how to modify it to power several BBBs. Finally, you were introduced to the network topology and the purpose of network switches. A short description about the used storage system used throughout this book ended this chapter.

If you interconnect everything as described in this chapter, it means that you have created the hardware basis of a super computer cluster.

In the next chapter, you will be learning in detail how to install the operating system and how to configure master and slave nodes. You will see how to configure a Samba share for external network storage as well as how to configure the SSH login for password-less remote key usage. I will guide you through the installation process of the required development tools and the creation of the first C/C++ applications. You will also be shown how to transfer data between the cluster and your LAN using FTP or SSH.

# 3
# Operating System Setup and Configuration

After you have set up the hardware of your cluster, you can bring it alive by installing the operating system. This chapter will guide you through the process of installing Linux and configuring all the required hardware links between the cluster nodes. It will teach you the differences between the master and the slave node and how to configure remote access and external network storage. For file sharing, Samba will be used, which is well known among Linux users. The first steps will be executed in an already existing Linux environment. If you don't have one, you can download Knoppix, Ubuntu, or other distributions and boot your PC or laptop from CD or DVD. If you don't have a CD or DVD drive in your laptop, you can prepare a USB stick and boot from that instead. Instructions on how to do this can be found at `http://www.ubuntu.com/download/desktop/create-a-usb-stick-on-windows`.

This system will be called a host environment in this chapter. As a step-by-step guide, the following points will be explained in the chapter:

- A description of the Linux host environment
- Downloading Ubuntu for ARM and creating the installation image for the master node
- Installing the OS on the master node
- Using an existing Samba share to create a common storage place for files and data
- Creating the installation image for slave nodes

- Configuring the shared folder's auto-mount function for slave nodes
    - Creating SSH login keys
    - Installing developer tools and an introduction to creating C/C++ applications
- Possibilities of how to transfer data between the master node and any remote computer

The first step is to provide a basic Linux operating system as the host environment. The upcoming section will provide you with an example.

 To write microSD cards on your host platform, it might be necessary to have an adapter from a microSD to normal SD format or a USB reader for microSD cards.

# The Linux host environment

The Linux host environment provides you with a basic platform for the easy creation of installation images. Actually, it is not necessary to use Linux. and you can also create bootable microSD cards from within other operating systems. However, creating the master installation image on the microSD card won't be different compared to copying the installation image onto the nodes' internal eMMC memory. Thus, for the sake of simplicity, a Linux environment is highly recommended. Another point of view is that Linux only does what you tell it to do. If you tell it to overwrite every single byte on the card with the contents of a binary file, it will do so, and the command is very simple. On Windows, you need very specialized software for such a task.

# Creating the master node's installation image

Here, we will guide you through the process of creating the installation image for your cluster's master node. First, you need to download the cluster operating system you want to use and copy it to a bootable microSD card. Afterwards, you can boot up your master node with the microSD card and either copy the OS to its internal memory or continue using the microSD card for operation. This book will use the second approach and use a 16 GB microSD card for additional swap space. Let's first start with a short introduction to bootable SD cards.

# Bootable SD cards and partition tables

There are some vendors who announce that their cards are bootable and others might not be. This is simply not true. Every microSD card and every memory stick is bootable. The only thing that has to be done is to create the correct partition table in the master boot record.

To give an example, let's assume that your SD card is inserted into your computer running your Linux host environment and the Linux kernel has access to the memory device through the /dev/sdc device path. Then, there might exist several partitions within this block device called /dev/sdc1, /dev/sdc2, and so on. Memory devices smaller than 2.1 TB are usually partitioned in the standard way using a partition table saved in the so-called **master boot record** (**MBR**). This is also the format used on BBB. The partition table is a list that contains a list of up to four partitions on the memory device. Besides this, the MBR also contains a code that is responsible for loading the boot sector of the bootable partition. The bootable partition is a special partition that has its bootable flag set. This is a byte that tells the master boot record that it is bootable and it has to load its first sector called the boot sector or **volume boot record** (**VBR**). This system has been invented by IBM and was used on the original IBM PC and has also existed in variations previously. Linux uses a special software that can be installed onto the MBR or the VBR in order to load their kernel, which is the core component of the operating system. An example of such a software is **Grand Unified Bootloader** (**GRUB**) or U-Boot, as it is used in BBB (visit http://en.wikipedia.org/wiki/Das_U-Boot). In this book, we will use a standard Linux image file that already contains all the required partitioning in the boot and filesystem partition. The only thing you have to do is write it onto a microSD card.

> There are different classes of microSD cards. The higher the class, the faster the cards are. It is a good idea to invest in getting a faster card in order to improve your system's performance. The number is the minimum guaranteed write speed in MB/s.

# Downloading Ubuntu for ARM

In this book, we will use the Ubuntu Linux distribution. To download a compatible version of Ubuntu, you can visit http://www.armhf.com/boards/beaglebone-black/#precise. *Precise* stands for Version 12.04, which is a version with long time support and gives you 5 years of guaranteed software package updates. On the ARMhf page, you can find different Ubuntu versions and each comes in three parts as follows:

- The root filesystem partition
- The Linux header files (for programming)
- The boot loader partition

There is also a link installation instruction, which will guide you through the installation process. If you use a newer version, you might have to update other packages as well, and it might become difficult to get a working system in the end. For this book, I have tested a working installation based on Ubuntu 12.04. Formerly, there was a file on the website mentioned previously, called `ubuntu-12.04-armhf-minfs-3.8.13-bone18.img.xz`, which simplifies the installation process and is available for download from the Packt Publishing website (`http://www.packtpub.com`). Once you have downloaded the file, you can create an installation image on the microSD card.

# Writing the installation image to the microSD card

If you downloaded a newer version of Ubuntu than the one described in this book or even another distribution, you should follow the installation instructions of the corresponding provider of the files. If you use the file provided with this book, you can simply follow the instructions given in this section. Although they might not be exactly the same with different versions, the installation will roughly follow the same scheme, regardless of the exact version. The installation process can be divided into the following steps:

- Extracting the compressed installation image
- Writing the binary image onto the microSD card
- Expanding the filesystem to use the full microSD card size

The last step is optional and only useful if the microSD card size is larger than the installation image. For example, if you bought a 16 GB microSD card (which is the maximally supported memory size), you can expand the 2 GB partition of the image to fit the size of the card. Then, you have more memory available and can, for example, save the current partition of BBB before overwriting it with another operating system. Or, you can keep multiple installation images on the microSD card. In this book, we will create a bootable 16 GB microSD card with a swap file for the master node. There is no great difference between using a swap file or a swap partition. In both cases, the operating system has to write to a slower memory type and the extra time required by the filesystem to access the swap file is negligible. The advantage of a swap file is that you can easily adapt its size and switch it on or off at your convenience.

Now, let's start with the first step of creating our bootable image for the master node.

 From now on, it will be assumed that you have a running Linux system from where you can execute commands and have access to the microSD card under /dev/mmcblk0.

To unpack the image file, you have to use the tar command, which should be available on any Linux operating system. Use the following command to extract the .xz file and get to the binary .img file:

```
tar -xJf ubuntu-12.04-armhf-minfs-3.8.13-bone18.img.xz
```

Alternatively, you can use the following:

```
tar -xf ubuntu-12.04-armhf-minfs-3.8.13-bone18.img.xz
```

 You need at least 2 GB of free space on your host environment and a microSD card for this.

The next step is to copy the image file onto the microSD card. Insert the microSD card into a USB card reader or whatever you need on your Linux host environment, and type the following command to write the image file to the microSD card:

```
sudo dd if=ubuntu-12.04-armhf-minfs-3.8.13-bone18.img of=/dev/mmcblk0
```

 Please make sure that of= specifies the correct memory device. Otherwise, you might render an existing filesystem useless.

This will copy the binary image and you can sit down and relax for around 10 to 20 minutes until the process is finished. The time required depends on the speed of your memory card and the card reader interface. At this point, you already have a working bootable microSD card. However, do not eject the card yet, as we will adapt it further in the next section.

 To visualize the copy progress, you can use the pv program. Download it with the following:

```
sudo apt-get install pv
```

You can then modify the preceding copy command as well as other dd commands:

```
pv ubuntu-12.04-armhf-minfs-3.8.13-bone18.img | sudo dd
  of=/dev/mmcblk0
```

# Adapting the image size to the card space

As we most probably have a card larger than 2 GB, we want to adapt the size of our filesystem partition to the size of the microSD card. To do this, we first have to make Linux read in the partition table that has been created by our preceding dd command. Type the following:

```
sudo partprobe
```

This will cause the Linux kernel to reread the partition table and update its virtual filesystem, which is /dev.

In the next step, we will run the partition program fdisk to adapt the partition size. The trick is to first delete the partition that will only cause the corresponding entry of the master boot record to vanish. Afterwards, we recreate the entry with a new size, which will lead to a new partition with the old filesystem that is still incorrect in size. The last and final step is to resize the file system. So, to resize an existing partition, the following works:

- Unmount the partition if it is mounted
- Delete the partition (not its content)
- Recreate the partition (without formatting!)
- Resize the existing filesystem
- Remount the partition

As we did not mount our newly created partition previously, it does not need to be unmounted. We can immediately start with deleting the second partition of the microSD card by typing the following:

```
sudo fdisk /dev/mmcblk0
```

Delete the second partition by pressing *D* and then pressing 2. Finally, create a new partition by pressing *N*, select the primary partition by pressing *P*, and take the default values that have all the space allocated for the new second partition. Press *W*, and then press *Q* to write the table and then exit the program. Afterwards, you have to reread the partition table again by typing the following:

```
sudo partprobe
```

Finally, the filesystem has to be resized to fit the new partition size:

```
sudo resize2fs /dev/mmcblk0p2
```

Now you have a working bootable microSD card with its whole memory space available. The next section will describe the installation of the newly created operating system on BBB.

# Installing the operating system on the master node

If you do not want to boot from BBB's internal memory, you have to keep in mind that it will use its first boot code to boot from the internal card or external card, if inserted. If the Linux partition on the external card differs from the internal memory, BBB will crash. To prevent it from crashing you have to activate the second boot code in order to boot from the external card by pressing the boot-selection button. As this is annoying, the better solution is to write the installation image into the internal memory as well. This will update the boot sector of the internal memory, which will automatically boot our external memory card without the need to press the boot-selection button.

If you have adapted the installation image to the size of your memory card that is larger than the internal eMMC memory of your BBB, you can copy the original .img file onto the microSD card, producing an image within an image. This is quite helpful because you can then boot the large image that contains the image of the correct memory size, which you can then copy directly to BBB's internal eMMC memory.

On your host environment, type the following:

```
mkdir ~/ubimage
sudo mount /dev/mmcblk0p2 ~/ubimage
```

This will create a temporary folder called ubimage and mount the second partition with the filesystem of our microSD card onto it.

Change the current directory to your download location of the system image file:

```
cd ~
```

Here, it is assumed that you have downloaded it to your home directory.

Now, copy the original installation image file into the predefined home directory of our recently mounted filesystem:

```
cp ubuntu-12.04-armhf-minfs-3.8.13-bone18.img ~/ubimage/home/ubuntu
```

 With the Ubuntu system used in this book, the standard username is ubuntu and the password is ubuntu. Thus, the home directory is also called ubuntu.

Do not unmount the filesystem yet; we will adopt the network configuration in the following section.

# Configuring the network interface

Still mounted on the host environment, the configuration files of the installation image can easily be adopted. To provide a network configuration that is compatible with your LAN network, you have to use a fitting IP address and net mask. To have Internet access on your BBBs, you have to provide a gateway as well. It is a good idea to use a static IP address, which means that every board will have its own IP address that will never change inside your LAN. This makes it easier to track down any errors in the future and identify boards by their IP. To alter the network configuration, you have to edit the /etc/network/interfaces file. There is a very nice utility called the midnight commander, which is a file-manager equivalent of the old Norton Commander from the MS-DOS era. It contains a simple and easy-to-use text editor that can be started by the mcedit command. You can install it in Ubuntu by typing the following:

```
sudo apt-get install mc
```

Having the midnight commander installed or any other editor of your choice, the next step is to edit the network configuration file of our still-mounted microSD card file system by typing the following:

```
sudo mcedit ~/ubimage/etc/network/interfaces
```

Change the corresponding lines to the following:

```
iface eth0 inet static
address 192.168.0.16
netmask 255.255.255.0
gateway 192.168.0.222
```

Save the file by pressing *F2*, and exit mcedit by pressing *F10*.

In this book, it is assumed that your LAN IP addresses start with 192.168.0. and your standard gateway is 192.168.0.222. The gateway can be your Internet router, for example. You might have to change these values to meet your needs. The netmask should always be 255.255.255.0. Some explanations on the IP numbering in local networks can be found at http://www.arrowmail.co.uk/articles/iprange.aspx.

Now, let's consider this scenario: you insert the microSD card with this network configuration into BBB. It will boot up and the Linux kernel will detect the network device of BBB, giving it the name `eth0` and saving its MAC address into its `udev` configuration file. If you use the same microSD card with another BBB later, then the kernel will detect a different network card and give it the name `eth1` instead of `eth0`. Because of this, the network configuration will fail to work because it assumes the name `eth0` instead of `eth1`. To prevent this from happening, the hardware detection rules have to be adapted. You can do so by editing the `~/ubimage/etc/udev/rules.d/70-presistent-net.rules` file and delete all lines that begin with the `SUBSYSTEM` keyword. Afterwards, you have to add the following line:

```
SUBSYSTEM=="net", ACTION="add", DRIVERS=="?*",
ATTR{address}=="*:*:*:*:*:*", ATTR{dev_id}=="0x0", ATTR{type}="1",
KERNEL="eth*", NAME="eth0"
```

 The preceding configuration line *must* be written without a line break.

This will cause the Linux kernel to always give the name `eth0` to any network device that it detects. This is only possible because BBB does not have more than one network device. If you add a USB WLAN stick, you might face a problem with this configuration.

Another thing we want to change is the hostname of our master node. I called mine gatekeeper because it acts like a gateway to the whole cluster, and all other cluster nodes should only be reachable through the master node. Changing the hostname is quite easy. Just edit the `~/ubimage/etc/hostname` file.

This file contains the hostname. Finally, we can unmount the microSD card's filesystem from our host environment by typing the following:

```
sudo umount /dev/mmcblk0p2
```

# Flashing the internal eMMC

As we have a bootable microSD card that will always assign the IP address `192.168.0.16` to any BBB it is inserted into, we can select our master node and boot it up with this card. Insert the microSD card into your master node and start it up with network cables attached.

[  Please keep in mind that you have to press the boot-selection button before you power up the device and hold it pressed until you see the blue LEDs flickering. ]

Once you have successfully booted up your master node, you can use any remote PC to log in via SSH. In your host environment, type the following:

```
ssh ubuntu@192.168.0.16
```

You will be asked for a password, which is `ubuntu`. Now you should see Linux's prompt change to the following:

```
ubuntu@gatekeeper:~$
```

This means that you have successfully logged in to your master node from a remote PC.

Once you have booted BBB from the external microSD card, the internal memory is reachable by `/dev/mmcblk1` and the microSD card is `/dev/mmcblk0`. Assuming that you followed the steps described previously, you should now have the original installation image in your home directory, which is `/home/ubuntu`. You can flash it now into the internal eMMC memory by issuing this command:

```
sudo dd if=~/ubuntu-12.04-armhf-minfs-3.8.13-bone18.img
 of=/dev/mmcblk1
```

This took 984 seconds on my BBB.

[  Please do not mix up `mmcblk0` and `mmcblk1`, otherwise you will overwrite your microSD card. ]

# The external network storage

When executing multiprocessor applications, every CPU must have access to any software library required. As every CPU means every BBB in our case, every BBB must have access to the same software libraries. If we store those libraries locally, this would:

- Waste a lot of memory
- Cause a lot of work if we update something, because we would have to update every single node
- Generate error sources because some nodes might have other versions installed, leading to inconsistency

To avoid these problems, an external network storage can be used. In this book, we will use a shared Samba folder. Samba can be easily installed on any Linux operating system. Ports for other OSes are also available. You can visit www.samba.org for more information.

In the following text, we will assume that you have a working Samba share on a server in your LAN with the following configuration:

```
[MPIShare]
comment = MPIShare
browseable = yes
readonly = no
valid users = ubuntu
path = /any_path_you_want_on_your_smb_server
```

This will create a Samba share, which is accessible by the user ubuntu, who is the default user regarding our installation image.

Now, the idea is that the samba server will act as a global network storage that will hold all the required files that have to be shared between remote PCs and all the cluster nodes. Because we want a logical hierarchy and do not allow any node except the master node to access this share directly, we will create a second Samba share coming from the master node that will do nothing but forward the share of our network storage. This way, we have a logically better-structured system. As mentioned in the previous chapter, this will not affect the performance of calculations on the cluster.

On the master node, type the following:

```
sudo apt-get update
sudo apt-get install samba smbfs
```

This will install Samba and the Samba filesystem on your master node. Then, you have to configure the master node so that it will automatically mount the network storage into its local filesystem. For this purpose, you first have to install the cifs-utils package, which will provide the required filesystem type in order to mount Samba shares:

```
sudo apt-get install cifs-utils
```

Next, create a directory with the following command:

```
sudo mkdir /var/mpishare
```

This will be the directory where the network share will be mapped to. Then, you have to modify the `/etc/fstab` file to add a line for the automount procedure:

```
//192.168.0.77/MPIShare /var/mpishare cifs
    credentials=/etc/credentials,gid=1000,uid=1000,auto 0 0
```

The `uid` and `gid` parameters will simulate these user and group identities when logging into the network storage server, respectively. The `MPIShare` directory name has to match the Samba configuration name inside the square brackets. The `/etc/credentials` file on the master node will be used to provide a username and password to log in. It contains the following two lines that describe a valid user login on the network storage server:

```
username=ubuntu
```

```
password=ubuntu
```

Modify this according to your Samba configuration on your network storage server. Finally, we configure Samba on the master node in order to forward the share to any slave node. Edit the `/etc/samba/smb.conf` file on your master node and modify the following lines:

```
[global]
hosts allow = 192.168.0.*
server string = Gatekeeper MPI Share
interfaces = 192.168.0.16/255.255.255.0
bind interface only = yes
```

In the section ###### Authentication ######, please modify the following:

```
security = user
guest account = nobody
null passwords = yes
```

Finally, at the end of the file, add the following:

```
[MPIShare2]
writable = yes
path = /var/mpishare
public = yes
guest ok = yes
guest only = yes
guest account = nobody
browsable = yes
```

This will enable the Samba server on the master node to share the previously mounted `/var/mpishare` folder to any slave nodes.

# Installing and configuring the slave nodes

Configuring the slave nodes is actually the same as configuring the master node, except that we do not need a Samba server on it. Instead, we have to configure the automount to mount the share of the master node. Also, we have to modify the network configuration.

## Creating the slave node's installation image

The slave nodes will not be booted from external microSD cards. Instead, the operating system will be booted from internal eMMC memory. To install Ubuntu into the internal eMMC, you can create an installation card exactly as described for the master node. The only difference is that your memory card must match the internal eMMC memory. Let's assume that you have the old BBB version with 2 GB internal memory. Then, you need a 2 GB installation image that is already provided with this book. On your host environment, copy the decompressed .img image file onto the microSD card by issuing the same command as the one described for the master node:

```
sudo dd if=ubuntu-12.04-armhf-minfs-3.8.13-bone18.img of=/dev/mmcblk0
```

Once you have done this, you have to configure the network configuration for the slave node's installation image.

## Configuring the slave node's network interface

You can use the same directory as the one used previously to mount the previously created installation image onto the filesystem of your host environment. Then, you have to edit the ~/ubimage/etc/network/interfaces file again and change the IP address to a unique address that you do not need in your whole LAN configuration, for example, 192.168.0.253.

Then, edit ~/ubimage/etc/hostname and give it a unique hostname, such as slaveinstaller. Also, change ~/ubimage/etc/udev/rules.d/70-presistent-net.rules as before.

Afterwards, you have to create the automount entry for the Samba share. Edit `~/ubimage/etc/fstab` and add the following line:

```
//192.168.0.16/MPIShare2 /var/mpishare cifs guest 0 0
```

Do not forget to create the `~/ubimage/var/mpishare again` directory. This provides you with an easy-to-use installation microSD card with which you can flash every single slave node.

# Flashing the internal eMMC

As done before, we can now boot the slave node with the slave node installation microSD card by holding the boot-selection button and powering up the board. Having booted from the external microSD card, we can flash the internal eMMC almost the same way as before by issuing this command:

```
sudo dd if=/dev/mmcblk0 of=/dev/mmcblk1
```

The only difference is that we copy the microSD card completely onto the internal eMMC instead of using a file on the microSD card. Next, reboot the board without the microSD card and log in via `ssh` from your host environment by issuing this command:

```
ssh ubuntu@192.168.0.253
```

Enter the password `ubuntu`. Now you should be logged in and the prompt should change to the following:

```
ubuntu@slaveinstaller:~$
```

Please issue the update command for `apt-get`:

```
sudo apt-get update
```

You have to think of a system that orders your cluster nodes. I use a straight enumeration of my boards regarding their names and IP addresses. The following table gives you an example of how to do this:

| Hostname | IP address |
|---|---|
| gatekeeper | 192.168.0.16 |
| beowulf1 | 192.168.0.17 |
| beowulf2 | 192.168.0.18 |
| beowulf3 | 192.168.0.19 |
| ... | ... |

Change `/etc/hostname` and `/etc/network/interfaces` according to your taste. You can easily repeat this procedure for every single slave node you add to your system.

## Creating SSH login keys

One thing that is required in order to enable all nodes to effectively work together is to simplify the SSH login process from the master node to all slave nodes. To accomplish this, we have to create a login key that makes passwords obsolete.

 For the following tutorial, let's assume that you have the following configuration: `192.168.0.16` is your master node with the name `gatekeeper` and `192.168.0.17` is your first slave node with the name `beowulf1`.

First, you want to enable your SSH login without a password but with only the authorization key from the gatekeeper to your node. Thus, log in to your master node and create an RSA key:

`ubuntu@gatekeeper:~>ssh-keygen -t rsa`

Answer all the following questions by pressing *Enter*. Do not create a password for the key. Now use `ssh` to create the `~/.ssh` directory on the `beowulf1` node:

`ubuntu@gatekeeper:~>ssh ubuntu@192.168.0.17 mkdir -p .ssh`

You are asked for the user password; enter it. Finally, append the new public key to the node's authorized keys:

`ubuntu@gatekeeper:~> cat .ssh/id_rsa.pub | ssh ubuntu@192.168.0.17 'cat >> .ssh/authorized_keys'`

Enter the password for the last time. In the future, you (and the master node in general) can SSH into your node from the gatekeeper without giving the password.

## A crash course in developing applications

The aim of this section is to provide you with a short crash course in programming on Linux operating systems. However, it is not possible to deal with this topic in all its glory. It takes years to get the hang of it and write good programs. However, this section tries to provide you with a basis you can build upon. If you want to get more detail on this topic, there is a lot of information on the Internet.

As you might not have developed applications previously, this section will give you a short introduction to this topic. As we have already seen in *Chapter 1, BeagleBone Black System Board,* in the *Software programming* section, there is a certain set of tools that have to be used with the source code in order to generate a binary file that can be executed — the actual program. Let's first see how this toolchain is actually installed.

# Installing development tools

Now that we have our cluster system running the operating system and the basic network configuration, we are ready to install the development tools. They enable us to write applications for our system.

To install the development tools on all nodes, first begin on the master node by issuing this command:

```
sudo apt-get install autotools-dev g++ build-essential gfortran
```

This will install the packages required to write applications. They will be used to compile the libraries that are later used to perform mathematical computations on the cluster. Now you can use `ssh` to repeat the same command for all the other cluster nodes. As you have distributed an SSH key, this is now simplified. On your master node, type the following:

```
ssh -t beowulf1 'sudo apt-get install autotools-dev g++
    build-essential gfortran'
```

This will install the toolchain on the first node called `beowulf1`. The `-t` option means that `ssh` will allocate a virtual console that allows us to input the root password for the slave node on the master node.

# First test program

To write a first program, log in to your master node and choose the proper directory for your experiments. Usually, this will be in your home directory. So, after you are logged in, you can create a folder called `test1`, for example, and enter it:

```
ubuntu@gatekeeper:~$ mkdir test1
ubuntu@gatekeeper:~$ cd test1
ubuntu@gatekeeper:~/test1$
```

Now that we are in the `test1` directory, we can start and edit our first source file. We will use the editor of the midnight commander that simplifies things and even has syntax highlighting:

```
ubuntu@gatekeeper:~/test1$ mcedit main.cpp
```

This will open a new file called `main.cpp`, which is our primary source file, as its name already says.

Let's start with the following example code:

```
int main() {

    return 0;
}
```

We press *F2* and then exit with pressing ESC twice or F10 once. Now we can compile this program by typing the following:

```
ubuntu@gatekeeper:~/test1$ c++ main.cpp
```

When you perform a directory listing now, you will see the following files:

```
ubuntu@gatekeeper:~/test1$ ls -l
total 12
-rwxrwxr-x 1 ubuntu ubuntu 7761 Jul  8 21:43 a.out
-rw-rw-r-- 1 ubuntu ubuntu   29 Jul  8 21:40 main.cpp
```

As you can see, the `a.out` file already has an **x-flag,** which stands for executable. So, `a.out` is already a lined program that can be executed by the Linux operating system. The `c++` command we typed previously has already executed the linker after the compilation. All programs will be called `a.out` by the linker by default. You can either rename it afterwards, or you can specify the output file you want by typing the following:

```
c++ -o test1 main.cpp
```

Please keep in mind that `-o` is a parameter that expects its value before the source code file. This means that you have to specify the target file first and then the source file. The preceding command will produce the same result as before, except that the output file is now simply called `test1`.

Now that we have successfully compiled our program, we can execute it. For this, we have to specify the filename of the program along with its path. Type the following command to run the program:

```
./test1
```

Nothing happens. This is because we didn't tell our program to do something visible. Let's take a closer look at the source code.

The first line, which is `int main() {`, means that we start a function called `main` that does not expect any parameters (so, there is nothing between the two round brackets), and the `int` keyword means that this function returns an integer value that is 4 bytes in size, in other words, a quad word. The range for such a value goes from $-2^{31}$ to $2^{31}-1$ (2 to the power of 31), giving a total of $2^{32}-1$ possibilities. The main function is the standard entry point for any program, and the linker tells the operating system where to find it. The contents of a function are encapsulated by curly braces that define a logical block of code. Each code statement must be ended by a semicolon.

The code line is as follows:

```
return 0;
```

This means that this function will return the value `0`. This value is directly returned to the operating system after the program is finished. To view this value, we can use this command:

```
echo $?;
```

The shell variable `$?` contains the return value of the last executed program. To try this, we change the return value of our program to something different, for example, 44. So, change the last line of the main function to the following:

```
return 44;
```

Save it and recompile the program. Then, you can execute it and view the return value with the following:

```
ubuntu@gatekeeper:~/test1$ ./test1
ubuntu@gatekeeper:~/test1$ echo $?;
44
ubuntu@gatekeeper:~/test1$
```

Congratulations, you have seen the output of your first C++ program.

Now you have seen how to practically develop C++ programs. Of course, there are many more things to know regarding libraries, including files, and so on. We will get back to this topic later when introducing the message-passing interface, which is OpenMPI, in *Chapter 4, Parallel Computing with OpenMPI and ScaLAPACK*.

# Transferring files from and to the BeagleBone master node

Of course, it will be necessary to back up your code and other files or simply transfer anything you want between a remote computer and the cluster's master node. There are different ways through which you can accomplish this. The easiest way is to use the Samba share that you have already configured.

However, you can use other ways such as **file transfer protocol** (**FTP**), of course.

# The FTP server

For secure FTP server functionality, you can install the `vsftpd` package, which stands for **very secure ftp daemon**. This is a package that was created in order to provide a very secure version of the FTP server software. You can install it by typing the following:

```
sudo apt-get install vsftpd
```

I got an error message after this, but I just repeated the command and it finished successfully. After the installation and configuration process, the server is started automatically. By default, the server is anonymous, which means that it does not allow any user to log in except "anonymous", who does not have any file rights.

The next step is to edit the `/etc/vsftpd.conf` configuration file by issuing the following command:

```
sudo mcedit /etc/vsftpd.conf
```

Now, uncomment the `#local_enable=YES` line by removing #, which will enable access for all users who are registered as local users on the master node. Now we have to restart the server daemon by typing this command:

```
sudo restart vsftpd
```

This is always required when you change the configuration file. After the daemon has restarted, you are able to log in to your master node using any FTP client. A nice gimmick is to change the banner of your FTP server by changing the line in /etc/vsftpd.conf to anything you want:

```
ftpd_banner=
```

This string will then be displayed in FTP clients such as FileZilla after the login:

```
Status:   Connecting with 192.168.0.16:21...
Status:   Connection established, waiting for welcome message...
Answer:   220 Welcome to your beagle bone beowulf cluster FTP server.
```

# File transfer with WinSCP

Another possibility that transfers files over the network is the **Secure Copy Protocol (SCP)**. It is similar to the FTP or SFTP protocol, but it is based on Secure Shell (SSH). This means that it is not necessary to install any FTP server early on, as SSH is a standard component of the Linux operating system.

A straightforward and easy-to-use program for Microsoft (R) Windows (TM) is WinSCP. You can download it from http://winscp.net/eng/download.php. The fastest way is to use the portable executable from the upper download section. Once you have started SCP, select the SCP protocol and enter your login data.

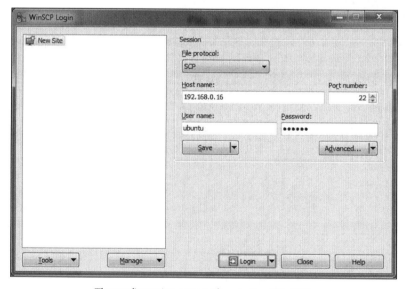

The configuration screen after starting WinSCP

Once WinSCP is started, it looks very similar to Midnight or Norton Commander, thus enabling you to easily manage your files.

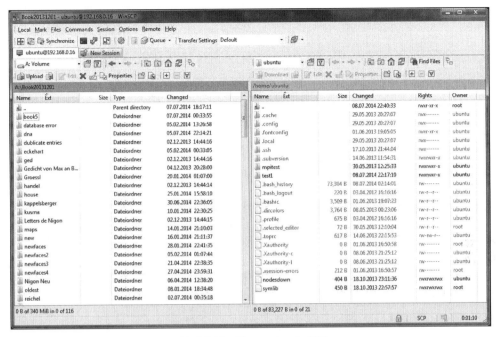

WinSCP for file transfer via SSH

In this file-management window, you can easily drag-and-drop your files from and to your BBB. This is just an example and you can use whichever tool you like.

# Summary

In this chapter, I showed you how to install the operating system on your BBBs. You learned about the small differences between configuring the master and slaves nodes. Additionally, I showed you how to write smaller system images to larger memory cards and how to adapt the filesystem size to use the full card size.

Examples of a network configuration were given to provide a basic system setup. This included the configuration of SSH, which is a powerful console tool that executes commands on your BBB from a remote location.

After a step-by-step guide on how to install the basic programming environment, you were given an example of how to write your first application in Linux on your BBB.

The chapter ended by configuring some additional tools such as FTP and Samba, and you were shown how to access and transfer files from and to your cluster.

# 4
# Parallel Computing with OpenMPI and ScaLAPACK

The advantage of a cluster compared to a normal personal computer is its capability of performing tasks in parallel and thereby reducing the overall calculation time. On modern computer platforms, there are two main architectures that perform parallel computations:

- Shared memory systems
- Distributed memory systems

On the shared memory system architecture, different CPUs or CPU cores share the same main memory. This means that every program that is loaded from one core or CPU can principally be used by other cores or CPUs as well. To optimally use such a system, the memory or process management has to take care that two processes do not access the same locations of the shared main memory at the same time. Otherwise, one process might have to wait for another until it has completed its operation or freed some locked resources. Also, software programmers have to take care of the fact that only one process can alter such memory areas at a time; otherwise, one process might invalidate the data of another process without its knowledge.

On distributed memory systems, however, every CPU or logical node has its own main memory. This way, one node cannot interfere with other nodes. The advantage is that there is no waiting time for resources to be locked or unlocked, and there are no potential conflicts between parallel processes. The disadvantage, however, is that there is no common main memory that can be accessed by different processors or nodes, making it necessary to load the same software into each node's main memory. To accomplish this, there is a well-established standard called **Message Passing Interface (MPI)**, which takes care of internode communications and will be covered in this chapter.

Apart from the basic MPI system that allows several nodes to work together, there is also the need for additional libraries that enable the cluster to perform parallel computations. A very important library is ScaLAPACK, which provides linear algebra routines that are scalable. This means that the required amount of calculation time can be reduced by adding more nodes to the system, and the routines provide the possibility to optimally share the computational work between the nodes. This chapter will explain the installation and configuration of ScaLAPACK as well as its basic usage.

# MPI – Message Passing Interface

MPI stands for Message Passing Interface. As a software standard, it realizes the most important part of cluster intercommunication. It is the fundamental software layer upon which all program control and data communication is based. Although MPI defines a system with which the nodes of a cluster can communicate, it does not define the strict protocol with which this communication takes place. Despite this, every MPI implementation requires a standard application programming interface (API). In our case, MPI will make use of the TCP/IP protocol by sending data packets across the cluster's network backbone. The development of MPI began in 1992 and the following important key features, among others, were required:

- Peer-to-peer communication
- Global communication
- Implementation in C and Fortran77

These are included in the MPI 1.0 standard. Beginning with Version 2 of MPI, the following important features were added:

- Parallel data input and output
- Dynamic process management
- Access to other processes' memory
- Additional language implementation for C++ and Fortran90

The possibility of accessing the memory of other cluster nodes or processing data in parallel avoids the need for the large main memory on the controlling node because calculation results do not need to be collected on one single point in order to process them further. In this book, however, we will make use of the MPI 1.5 standard for software compatibility reasons.

# The process control

A very important feature of MPI is the process control. If you start cluster software that has to make use of several nodes in order to perform a calculation, the same software has to run on all the computational nodes accordingly. It would be unpractical if a user had to start the software on each node separately, so there is a very convenient system already incorporated in the MPI standard.

If you want to run a special MPI program, you have to perform the following:

- Use a special command called `mpirun`
- Specify the number of nodes you want to run the software on

For example, if you want to run a program called `test1` in the current directory on four nodes of your cluster, then you will type in the master node's console:

```
mpirun -n 4 ./test1
```

This command tells MPI that you want to start four processes that are automatically distributed on four nodes. If you have less than four nodes, one node will run more than a single process, which will decrease the system's performance considerably.

 If you start more processes on your cluster than the available nodes, one node will execute more than one process, and the overall system performance will decrease dramatically.

MPI will then look up a standard file that contains all nodes and their IP addresses. From this, it will use the given amount of nodes and try to execute the software on them. For this reason, several needs have to be met:

- The software has to be in the same location on each node
- The required libraries have to be installed on each node

To accomplish this, you were already shown how to configure a network share to hold that kind of software and its libraries. If this share is mounted to the same directory on every node, the MPI system can find all the required software.

Now, it also becomes clear why it was necessary to configure SSH to accept logins without passwords. This is important for the MPI process control that takes place from the master node to all the slave nodes that accept the key of the master node.

You will be given some simple examples in the next subsection after the installation and configuration of the OpenMPI subsystem; then, it will become clearer how the node intercommunication works and how data can be sent from one node to another.

# The software structure

As mentioned previously, every single program written for the cluster has to run on all nodes during a parallel operation. To ease this task, the software is loaded from a common network location. However, what does the structure of such software look like? There are many possibilities. The structure is based on the MPI standard, and the following steps have to be executed before any additional program code:

1. Initialize the local MPI subsystem.
2. Get the number of global MPI subsystems (nodes).
3. Get the rank of the local MPI subsystem.
4. Use MPI.
5. Finalize MPI on the program exit.

Step 1 initializes the MPI API that sets up any required internal configurations the user does not care about. In the next step, the number of processors or nodes is determined by the software. You have to keep in mind that the software structure described previously is run by all the nodes in the cluster. In order for each local software copy to determine its own identity, which means the node on which the software is actually running; step 3 gets the rank of the MPI process. The rank is a number that tells us whether we are on the master node (rank = 0) or a slave node (rank > 0). To be more specific, we can call an identification routine of the MPI API that will tell us the processor's name on which the software is running. This will be our node name. After these initial steps, we can make use of MPI. How exactly this works will be explained in the next subsection, which is *Creating a test application*.

The following diagram tries to summarize the basic concept of MPI. The networking backbone with the TCP/IP protocol and SSH interface provides the basic layer for the OpenMPI cluster communication. Software can be started by the master node and is automatically loaded from a shared network storage place into the slave nodes by the SSH and TCP/IP communication.

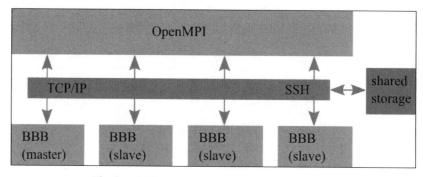

The OpenMPI system and communication structure

# Installing and configuring OpenMPI

The following subsection will guide you through the process of downloading and configuring the OpenMPI package in Ubuntu. It will also provide you with basic programming examples in order to create simple cluster applications and make you understand the basic usage and functioning of the MPI standard interface.

# Downloading and installing OpenMPI packages

Thankfully, OpenMPI is regarded as a standard package under Ubuntu Linux. You can download a precompiled version with the following command:

```
sudo apt-get install openmpi1.5-bin openmpi1.5-doc libopenmpi1.5-dev
```

Keep in mind that this has to be done on every single node. You can also execute commands using the `ssh` command from your master node.

For the following tutorial, let's assume that you have the following network setup:

- `192.168.0.16`: This is your master node with the name `gatekeeper`
- `192.168.0.17`: This is your first slave node with the name `beowulf1`
- `192.168.0.18`: This is your second slave node with the name `beowulf2`

I will show you how to set up MPI communication between these nodes. You can then repeat all the steps for every additional node.

In *Chapter 3, Operating System Setup and Configuration*, you already enabled SSH-login without the password but by only using the authorization key from the gatekeeper to your nodes. If you haven't, please refer to *Chapter 3, Operating System Setup and Configuration*, for how to do this. You were also shown how to use a common network share to create a common folder for each node. Please make sure that you have set the correct access rights to this folder. In my example, this is done with the following command:

```
sudo chown ubuntu:ubuntu /var/mpishare
```

> Please keep in mind that according to the configuration of the previous chapters, the slave nodes mount a forwarded network share from the master node. For this reason, the master node has to be booted up first. However, usually the slave nodes wait for the share to be available, and there should be no problem if you start all boards simultaneously.

# Configuring the default hostfile

In order to enable OpenMPI to find all the nodes of your cluster, you have to fulfill the following requirements:

- Add your hostnames to the master node's `resolv.conf`
- Add your hostnames to OpenMPI's default hostfile

The first point is not strictly required, as you can also work with IP addresses only. However, I prefer giving names to computers.

The master node's `resolv.conf` file works like a **domain name server (DNS)** on the local system. This enables the node to convert computer names into IP addresses. This means that if you use node names within your MPI hostfile, you also need to specify them in your master resolve configuration file, which is located at `/etc/resolv.conf`. An example of this file is as follows:

```
nameserver 192.168.0.222
gatekeeper 192.168.0.16
beowulf1 192.168.0.17
beowulf2 192.168.0.18
beowulf3 192.168.0.19
beowulf4 192.168.0.20
```

The `nameserver` in this case is identical with the gateway, which is my Internet router.

The next step is to add all your node names to your OpenMPI default hostfile. Do this by editing the `/etc/openmpi/openmpi-default-hostfile` file.

As a last step, you have to tell OpenMPI where this hostfile is located. This is done with the standard parameter configuration file, which is located at `/etc/openmpi/openmpi-mca-params.conf`.

Add or modify the following line:

```
orte_default_hostfile=/etc/openmpi/openmpi-default-hostfile
```

Congratulations, you have set up OpenMPI! In order to test your system interconnection and provide more insight into the working principles of OpenMPI, let's continue with some basic examples.

# Creating a test application

As we have already seen in the first chapter, we use a compiler to translate our program source code into machine language. Actually, nothing will change if we use OpenMPI, of course. However, we have to take care to correctly link the OpenMPI libraries to our program. We can do this by specifying parameters to the compiler. As these parameters might vary from system to system, a simpler way has been established. Instead of using the standard C++ compiler directly, we should use a compiler wrapper called **mpic++**. This is nothing else but an alias for the actual C++ compiler with additional parameters. It will take care to correctly add all the required stuff for the OpenMPI interface.

Let's first go into the network share path that is mounted to /var/mpishare on the master node. In the master node's console, create a folder named mpitest and go inside it:

**ubuntu@gateeper:/var/mpishare$ mkdir mpitest && cd mpitest**

In this directory, we create a file called mpitest.c with the following content:

```
#include <cstdlib>
#include <mpi.h>

int main(int argc, char* argv[])
{
    int numprocessors, rank, namelen;
    char processor_name[MPI_MAX_PROCESSOR_NAME];

    MPI_Init(&argc, &argv);
    MPI_Comm_size(MPI_COMM_WORLD, &numprocessors);
    MPI_Comm_rank(MPI_COMM_WORLD, &rank);
    MPI_Get_processor_name(processor_name, &namelen);

    if (rank==0)
    {
        std::cout << "Processor name: " << processor_name << "\n";
        std::cout << "master (" << rank << "/" << numprocessors <<
")\n";
    } else {
        std::cout << "Processor name: " << processor_name << "\n";
        std::cout << "slave (" << rank << "/" << numprocessors <<
")\n";
    }
    MPI_Finalize();

}
```

Let me first explain the code line by line.

The first included line makes the standard C library functions available. The second included line loads the OpenMPI API function definitions into the source code. The main function starts with the following:

```
int main(int argc, char* argv[])
```

This defines two parameters, which are `argc` and `argv`. The first one is an integer value that tells you the amount of command-line arguments. The second is an array of character pointers. These pointers give the memory location of continuously saved character strings that define the program command and the parameters passed to the program from the console command line at the startup. These arguments will also be passed to the `MPI_Init` function, which will be explained shortly. The next two lines are variable declarations:

```
int numprocessors, rank, namelen;
char processor_name[MPI_MAX_PROCESSOR_NAME];
```

We have three integer values for the number of processors available, the rank of the node this program is running on, and the maximum length of the processor's name (the node's name). The second line defines an array of characters that have a specific length set by a constant from MPI. Constants are usually written in capital letters. Finally, the initialization function of MPI is called and the two command-line arguments are passed:

```
MPI_Init(&argc, &argv);
```

The following three commands retrieve the configuration of the MPI system according to the environment we want the software to run in. This also depends on the start parameters given to `mpirun`, which will be explained in detail shortly.

```
MPI_Comm_size(MPI_COMM_WORLD, &numprocessors);
MPI_Comm_rank(MPI_COMM_WORLD, &rank);
MPI_Get_processor_name(processor_name, &namelen);
```

The first function call saves the number of processors into the `numprocessors` variable. The `&` sign before the variable tells the compiler to use the address of the variable instead of the reference. By passing an address, the memory location is passed instead of its value, thus enabling the function to alter the variable content globally. The first parameter `MPI_COMM_WORLD` is a constant that tells the `MPI_Comm_` functions where to send or retrieve information. In this case, the whole MPI environment with all specified nodes is used according to the `mpirun` command. This was the initialization part of the program.

This is followed by the main part of the program, which is a simple `if` branch in this example. This `if` branch looks for the rank of the software instance. For instance, we name the copy of the software that is executed on a specific node. Thus, each node executes one instance of the same software. By looking at the rank value, the `if` expression branches into the upper or the lower part. If the instance is running on the master node, the rank value is zero and the second output command starting with `std::cout` outputs a line that begins with the word `master`. If the instance is running on a slave node, the rank is not zero and the second output command outputs a line that begins with the word `slave`. The program ends with the `MPI_Finalize` command, which frees resources and tells the MPI system that this instance has ended.

Let's now compile the source code with the OpenMPI compiler wrapper. Enter the following command:

```
mpic++ mpitest.c -o mpitest
```

The C++ compiler wrapper, which is `mpic++`, passes additional parameters and link libraries to the standard C++ compiler. The corresponding wrapper for the C compiler cc is mpicc. The preceding command should create the `mpitest` file.

We can now start this program by just typing the following:

```
./mpitest
```

The output will then be the following:

```
Processor name: gatekeeper
master (0/1)
```

We can see only one processor with a rank of zero. This is because we did not use `mpirun` to start the program and thus the software was started on the master node only. If we want to run it on several nodes in parallel, for example, two nodes, we have to type the following:

```
mpirun -n 2 ./mpitest
```

The start of the program will take a little longer as the MPI system synchronizes the start of the instances and has to load the software on the other nodes. The output should be something like this:

```
Processor name: beowulf1
slave (1/2)
Processor name: gatekeeper
master (0/2)
```

As you can see, the output has doubled and the program was executed with two instances on two different nodes. The order of the nodes used by the `mpirun` command is the order of the entries in the `openmpi-default-hostfile` configuration file.

# Simple node synchronization

If you use even more nodes, such as eight in my example, the output can be mixed up as follows:

```
Processor name: gatekeeper
Processor name: beowulf2
Processor name: beowulf3
Processor name: beowulf1
slave (2/8)
slave (3/8)
slave (1/8)
master (0/8)
Processor name: beowulf6
Processor name: beowulf4
Processor name: beowulf7
Processor name: beowulf5
slave (5/8)
slave (6/8)
slave (4/8)
slave (7/8)
```

This is because all instances output in parallel and there is no synchronization between these instances. The output is forwarded as it comes. The order is dependent on the network package order, the network cable length, the exact frequency difference between two boards, and much more. For complex software, it becomes necessary to synchronize operations in order to avoid unforeseen problems. A very simple possibility is the use of the `MPI_Barrier` function. If one instance calls this function, the instance is paused until all other instances have also called this function. This leads to time synchronization between the cluster nodes.

# Passing values between nodes

Of course, we are missing one very important step in order to write software that can really use all these different nodes of our cluster: the data communication. There are two powerful functions, namely:

```
MPI_Send(void* data, int count, MPI_Datatype datatype, int
destination, int tag, MPI_Comm communicator);

MPI_Recv(void* data, int count, MPI_Datatype datatype, int source, int
tag, MPI_Comm communicator, MPI_Status* status);
```

The first one can send values via the MPI system, and the second one can receive values. Let's examine how these two functions can be applied in the following example program:

```cpp
#include <cstdlib>
#include <mpi.h>

using namespace std;

int main(int argc, char* argv[])
{
    int numprocessors, rank, namelen;
    char processor_name[MPI_MAX_PROCESSOR_NAME];

    MPI_Init(&argc, &argv);
    MPI_Comm_size(MPI_COMM_WORLD, &numprocessors);
    MPI_Comm_rank(MPI_COMM_WORLD, &rank);
    MPI_Get_processor_name(processor_name, &namelen);

    int number;

    if (rank==0)
    {
        number = -4;
        MPI_Send(&number, 1, MPI_INT, 1, 0, MPI_COMM_WORLD);
    } else {
  MPI_Recv(&number, 1, MPI_INT, 0, 0, MPI_COMM_WORLD,
 MPI_STATUS_IGNORE);
        cout << "I am " << processor_name << " and got " << number
    << " from node 0." << endl;
    }
    MPI_Finalize();
}
```

As you can see, the first part of if branch, which is executed only in the instance of the master node (rank == 0), will set the number variable to -4. After this, it calls the MPI_Send function with the address of the variable, followed by the count of how many of these variables we want to send. In our case, this is one. The next parameter, which is MPI_INT, tells OpenMPI that we want to send an integer value. The goal is the node number 1; the following zero is a special tag that we do not use in this example and the last parameter tells OpenMPI that communication has to take place over all the nodes specified by the mpiexec command. Let's save this code in mpitest2.c and compile it by typing the following:

```
mpic++ mpitest2.c -o mpitest2
```

Then, we execute it with the following:

```
mpirun -n 2 ./mpitest2
```

You should see the following output:

```
I am beowulf1 and got -4 from node 0.
```

If you start the program with more than two nodes, you will see the program hanging because all other nodes with a rank greater than 1 will wait for their data but will never receive them. This is because we only sent data to node number 1 with the MPI_Send command. We can easily cause the master node to send the number to all slave nodes by adding a loop over all processes. Take a look at this line:

```
    MPI_Send(&number, 1, MPI_INT, 1, 0, MPI_COMM_WORLD);
```

Change the preceding line to the following line:

```
    for (int i = 1; i < numprocessors; i++)
            MPI_Send(&number, 1, MPI_INT, i, 0, MPI_COMM_WORLD);
```

The i variable will then count from 1 to numprocessors - 1, causing all nodes specified by mpiexec to receive the number. Save this program to mpitest3.c and compile it. Say you have five slave nodes and start the program with the following:

```
mpiexec -n 6 ./mpitest3
```

Then, you will see the following output:

```
I am beowulf1 and got -4 from node 0.
I am beowulf2 and got -4 from node 0.
I am beowulf3 and got -4 from node 0.
I am beowulf4 and got -4 from node 0.
I am beowulf5 and got -4 from node 0.
```

Now, you have learned how to principally use OpenMPI to pass data between your cluster nodes. With some practice, you can write your first calculation software. Of course, there are already mighty mathematical libraries that can utilize OpenMPI. The following section will deal with ScaLAPACK, which is a scalable linear algebra library that solves typical linear mathematical problems.

# ScaLAPACK and linear mathematical problems

There are many types of linear mathematical problems in science and engineering. Even if a problem is more complicated, it can be linearized in many ways, providing a simplification and the possibility to use well-established linear solvers.

An example of a linear mathematical problem is the rotation of a vector. The rotation of a vector in three dimensions around a specific axis—for example, the z-axis—can be written in the following way:

$$\begin{pmatrix} x' \\ y' \\ z' \end{pmatrix} = \begin{pmatrix} \cos\alpha & \sin\alpha & 0 \\ -\sin\alpha & \cos\alpha & 0 \\ 0 & 0 & 1 \end{pmatrix} \begin{pmatrix} x \\ y \\ z \end{pmatrix}$$

Any point with the coordinates **x**, **y**, and **z** gets new coordinates **x'**, **y'** and **z'** when it is rotated by the angle alpha around the coordinate origin. The original point and the rotated point can both be described by vectors, and the rotation itself is described by a rotation matrix. By multiplying the original vector with the rotation matrix, we get the result vector. This is a simple example of a linear operation, which is the matrix-vector multiplication. Now, we can ask that if we have the rotated point and the rotation matrix, what was the original point? Of course, we know that the rotation just has to take place in the different direction, namely the negative angle. This corresponds to the task of solving the following linear problem:

$$b = Mx$$

Here, **b** is the given rotated vector, **M** is the given rotation matrix, and **x** is the unknown original vector. To solve this problem, we can use an existing library called LAPACK. **LAPACK** stands for **Linear Algebra Package**. It provides you with a complete set of functions that solve virtually any linear algebra problem.

In general problems, **M** is more complicated than a rotation, and the number of dimensions can be very huge. Consider that you want to analyze the movement of millions of mass points connected by springs; then, you can end up with a linear equation system with millions of unknowns. The solution of such a system on only one computer takes a long time. To speed up the process, you can use a powerful library called **ScaLAPACK**. It is the scalable version of LAPACK that can utilize MPI to distribute calculations onto our cluster nodes. ScaLAPACK is based on the BLAS, LAPACK, PBLAS, BLACS, and MPI libraries. To understand this bunch of software libraries and how they work together, have a look at the following diagram:

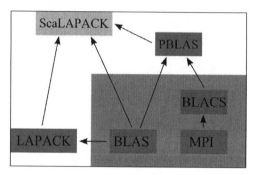

ScaLAPACK's components

The BLAS library contains all the basic linear algebra operations such as the matrix-vector or number-vector multiplications. LAPACK is then based upon BLAS and provides higher-level routines such as the solution of linear equations. BLACS is the communication layer that provides an interface for BLAS routines to use MPI. PBLAS then provides routines that can be executed in parallel on several nodes by combining BLAS and MPI via BLACS. The functionalities of these are then combined in ScaLAPACK in order to provide a powerful library that solves linear problems on clusters. The software implementation of the libraries in the red area is platform-dependent. BLAS is an especially important feature. The speed of any computation using ScaLAPACK depends on the speed of BLAS. If you install the standard reference BLAS package, you cannot expect calculations to be carried out by maximum performance. You will need to install a specially optimized package for your system or compile and adapt it yourself.

An example is Vesperix's ATLAS ARM, which you can get from
`http://www.vesperix.com/arm/atlas-arm/`.

# Installing and configuring ScaLAPACK

To install ScaLAPACK, you can download it from netlib at `http://www.netlib.org/scalapack/#_scalapack_version_2_0_2`.

Download the source tarball into a folder in your `/var/mpishare` directory, and extract it into a convenient directory, for example, `/var/mpishare/sca`. As ScaLAPACK depends on many different libraries, it might not be easy to compile it successfully. To simplify things, there is a handy setup script written in Python. You can download it from `http://www.netlib.org/scalapack/scalapack_installer.tgz`.

Extract the installer script into the source directory of ScaLAPACK. Then, you can run the script with the following command:

```
./setup.py --prefix=/var/mpishare/sca
--mpiincdir=/usr/include/mpi/ --downall
```

The `prefix` option tells the setup script where to install the ScaLAPACK libraries, which will be a subdirectory called `lib` below this folder. The `mpiincdir` command specifies the location of the OpenMPI include files, and the `downall` option tells the setup script to download the source code of any required libraries that are not found in your system.

> Compiling the packages and running the automatically started test suite takes a very long time (hours). To speed up the process, you can skip the test suite by specifying the `--notesting` parameter.

After the installation is complete, you should see some messages containing the following:

```
ScaLAPACK is installed.
Use it in moderation J
********************************************************
********************************************************
ScaLAPACK installation completed.
Your BLAS library is                      :
Your LAPACK library is                    :
Your BLACS/ScaLAPACK library is           : -L/var/mpishare/sca/lib/
-lscalapack
Log messages are in the
```

```
/var/mpishare/sca/build/log directory.
```

The ScaLAPACK testing programs are in:

```
/var/mpishare/sca/build/build/scalapack-2.0.0/TESTING
```

The `/var/mpishare/sca/build` directory contains the source code of the libraries

that have been installed. It can be removed at this time.

After the `BLACS/ScaLAPACK` library line, you will see the additional linker parameters that you have to add in order to compile a program using ScaLAPACK. The most important information is the location of the installed libraries. In our case, they were installed to `/var/mpishare/sca/lib/` because we specified `/var/mpishare/sca` as the destination prefix earlier.

The following library files have been created:

- `librefblas.a`: This is the reference BLAS library
- `libreflapack.a`: This is the reference LAPACK library
- `libscalapack.a`: This is the ScaLAPACK library including BLACS and PBLAS
- `libtmg.a`: This is a component of LAPACK providing generations of test matrices and used for timing tests

Besides the last library, all the libraries are required in order to build a working ScaLAPACK application. As a next step, we will build and run a well-known example program for C.

# Solving a positive symmetric tridiagonal system with ScaLAPACK

After the successful installation of the ScaLAPACK libraries, we can use our BeagleBone Black cluster to solve mathematical problems. The optimized usage of the ScaLAPACK library is very complicated, and functions are not easy to understand. The following example just provides a first look into its usage and tries to show us the basic utilization of ScaLAPACK functions. Also, function names are not easy to remember and there are higher-level libraries that we will get to know later, starting with the next chapter. They will considerably simplify the solution of mathematical problems without knowing all the ScaLAPACK functions in detail.

However, let's have a look how ScaLAPACK can be used to solve a linear problem on four cluster nodes first. The following example file was obtained from `http://acts.nersc.gov/scalapack/hands-on/etc/pdpttr_2/pdpttr_2.c.html`.

However, it cannot be compiled with our C compiler without making small changes. Mathematicians are not very fond of the programming languages C and C++ because there used to be a more practical language for them, for example, Fortran77. The reason is that Fortran77 already provides mathematical data types such as matrices that have to be artificially defined in C. For this reason, libraries such as ScaLAPACK naturally provide functions for Fortran. When we import these functions by linking the library to our C program, function names are different. The C compiler sees them with an underscore after the function names, which does not exist for the Fortran compiler. Because of this, we have to change some lines and add an underscore after the following function calls:

- Change `pdpttrf` in line 123 to `pdpttrf_`
- Change `pdpttrs` in line 128 to `pdpttrs_`
- Change `pdpttrf` in line 165 to `pdpttrf_`
- Change `pdpttrs` in line 170 to `pdpttrs_`

Save the modified source file to `/var/mpishare/scatest` and run the following build command in this directory:

```
mpicc scatest1.c  /var/mpishare/sca/lib/libscalapack.a
/var/mpishare/sca/lib/libreflapack.a /var/mpishare/sca/lib/librefblas.a
-lgfortran -o scatest1
```

As you can see, we have to add the three ScaLAPACK libraries to the compiler command line in order to link them together into one binary file. This is an example of a statically linked program. Because ScaLAPACK is designed for Fortran, it also requires some standard Fortran library that is added with the `-lgfortran` switch. The output is set to `scatest1`.

This program solves the following **tridiagonal** matrix equation:

$$\begin{pmatrix} 1.8180 & 0.8385 & 0 & 0 & 0 & 0 & 0 & 0 \\ 0.8385 & 1.6602 & 0.5681 & 0 & 0 & 0 & 0 & 0 \\ 0 & 0.5681 & 1.3420 & 0.3704 & 0 & 0 & 0 & 0 \\ 0 & 0 & 0.3704 & 1.2897 & 0.7027 & 0 & 0 & 0 \\ 0 & 0 & 0 & 0.7027 & 1.3412 & 0.5466 & 0 & 0 \\ 0 & 0 & 0 & 0 & 0.5466 & 1.5341 & 0.4449 & 0 \\ 0 & 0 & 0 & 0 & 0 & 0.4449 & 1.7271 & 0.6946 \\ 0 & 0 & 0 & 0 & 0 & 0 & 0.6946 & 1.3093 \end{pmatrix} x = b$$

Here, **b** is a complex vector, namely:

$$b = \begin{pmatrix} 1 + 8i \\ 2 + 7i \\ 3 + 6i \\ 4 + 5i \\ 5 + 4i \\ 6 + 3i \\ 7 + 2i \\ 8 + 1i \end{pmatrix}$$

As the matrix is real-valued, the problem can be split into real and imaginary parts. So, you can either see it as a complex valued problem or two independent real-valued problems.

The program has been written for four processes. Thus, we have to run it with the following:

```
mpirun -n 4 ./scatest1
```

The following output should then be produced:

```
MYPE=0: x[:] =   0.3002   0.5417   1.4942   1.8546

MYPE=1: x[:] =   1.5008   3.0806   1.0197   5.5692

MYPE=3: x[:] =   1.3090   1.2988   0.6563   0.4156

MYPE=2: x[:] =   3.9036   1.0772   3.4122   2.1837
```

## Understanding the code

To understand this solution, we have to know how the original data and calculation tasks were distributed between our four processes.

Let's first have a look at the structure of the program. It starts with some `#include` statements that import function and constant definitions. Take a look at the `extern` statements such as the following:

```
extern void Cblacs_get();
```

These statements import BLACS functions for MPI communication. With them, a process grid is defined and used, which will be explained shortly.

To simplify things, we first look at the BLACS call in line 78:

```
Cblacs_pinfo(&mype, &npe)
```

This will get information about our MPI system and return the process ID of this instance into a variable called mype and the total number of processes into a variable called npe. The next call is to the following:

```
Cblacs_get(0, 0, &context)
```

This saves the BLACS context into the variable named context. To understand this, we have to understand what a context is. A context in BLACS is nothing but a logical partitioning of our MPI communication space. It allows us to group processes into contexts and separate different groups from one another in order to avoid interference. It also allows us to create overlapping process groups, and each group defines a process grid that is used to parallelize math operations. Such a grid can be thought of being like a matrix with M rows and N cols where each element is a process or, in our case, a BeagleBone Black system (as we never want to start more processes than we have boards). In this context, consisting of all the MPI nodes this software was started on, the call to Cblacs_gridinit will initialize our process grid:

```
Cblacs_gridinit(&context, "R", 1, npe);
```

"R" stands for row major ordering. This specifies that we want our grid to be ordered by rows first, which is also the default value. The next parameter specifies the number of rows to be used (in our case, 1) and the number of columns (in our case, the value of npe).

Now, the program starts to distribute the data onto the process grid. It starts with the tridiagonal matrix by saving its diagonal elements (red) and extra diagonal elements (blue) into the two arrays, which are d[] and e[]. Processes 0 and 2 contain the left half of the matrix and processes 1 and 3 contain the right half. We will use two processes per half matrix to also distribute real and complex parts of our solution vector onto separate processes. Given this data distribution, the solution output we saw previously has to be interpreted in the following way:

$$x = \begin{pmatrix} MYPE0[0] + i\, MYPE2[0] \\ MYPE0[1] + i\, MYPE2[1] \\ MYPE0[2] + i\, MYPE2[2] \\ MYPE0[3] + i\, MYPE2[3] \\ MYPE1[0] + i\, MYPE3[0] \\ MYPE1[1] + i\, MYPE3[1] \\ MYPE1[2] + i\, MYPE3[2] \\ MYPE1[3] + i\, MYPE3[3] \end{pmatrix} = \begin{pmatrix} 0.3002 + 3.9036\, i \\ 0.5417 + 1.0772\, i \\ 1.4942 + 3.4122\, i \\ 1.8546 + 2.1837\, i \\ 1.5008 + 1.3090\, i \\ 3.0806 + 1.2988\, i \\ 1.0197 + 0.6563\, i \\ 5.5692 + 0.4156\, i \end{pmatrix}$$

The `mype` variable is used to identify the process number of the software instance. On instances 0 and 1, vector *b* is set to contain only its real values. On instances 2 and 3, vector *b* is set to contain only its imaginary values. As last step to set up a process, a so-called array descriptor for the distributed matrix has to be defined. It is used by ScaLAPACK to understand how the corresponding matrix portions are stored in the memory. The first descriptor is for matrix *A* and is set to the following:

```
[501, context_1, n, nb, 0, lda, 0]
```

The second descriptor is set for vector **b** and is set to the following:

```
[502, context_1, n, nb, 0, ldb, 0]
```

The first value determines the descriptor type. `501` and `502` are constants that stand for one-dimensional storage type. This is possible because we only have very few elements in our matrix that are nonzero. For more details, refer to the ScaLAPACK tutorials and references all over the Internet. The second value sets the context for the array. The software has created separate contexts: one for mype values 0 and 1 and another for mype values 2 and 3. This enables ScaLAPACK to logically divide calculation operations. The value of `n` gives you the number of rows and `nb` gives you the number of columns in this context. The following zero value is the blocking factor for column distribution and `ldb` is the blocking factor for row distribution. The last zero states the process row over which the first row of the matrix *A* and the vector *b* are distributed, respectively. Having set up all this stuff and some extra variables with free memory for working space, we can finally call two functions, namely `pdpttrf` and `pdpttrs`.

The `pdpttrf` command computes a Cholesky factorization of an N-by-N real tridiagonal symmetric positive definite distributed matrix *A*, and `pdpttrs` solves our equation system using the factorized matrix. It is not possible to go into all the mathematical details in this book, but the procedure can be explained in the following simplified manner.

# Understanding the mathematics behind the code

According to Cholesky, every symmetric and positive definite matrix *A* can be split into two factors:

$$A = LL^T$$

Here, $L$ is a lower triangular matrix, which means that all values above its diagonal are zero. This can be used to simplify the solution of a linear equation system. Say, we have this system:

$$Ax = b$$

Here, $A$ is a positive definite symmetric tridiagonal matrix and $x$ and $b$ are vectors; we can decompose $A$ according to Cholesky and get the following:

$$LL^T x = b$$

Now, we can define a new solution vector, $y$, to be the following:

$$y = L^T x$$

Solve this very simple equation:

$$Ly = b$$

This equation is very simple because $L$ is triangular, and it has one row where only one value is nonzero. Starting with this row, the first component of $b$ is already given. Knowing this component, the next row of $L$ leads to the next component of $b$, and so on. After knowing the value of $y$, $x$ can be found the same way by solving the following:

$$L^T x = y$$

# Summary

This chapter showed you the first steps into the world of parallel computations with ScaLAPACK on a BeagleBone Black cluster by distributing a problem between four cluster nodes.

To introduce you to this technique, the predominating computer architectures were explained in the beginning of the chapter, and you were introduced to the message-passing interface OpenMPI. OpenMPI is the basis for our BeagleBone Black cluster and provides the communication layer for data transfer between the cluster nodes. The chapter continued with providing an easy guide on how to install and configure OpenMPI on your BeagleBone Black boards. The MPI part of this chapter ended with some examples of how to use the API to transfer simple integer values between the cluster nodes.

To introduce you to the mathematical computations, the chapter continued with the installation procedure for ScaLAPACK, where you learned how to download and compile free library source code. Although it is not possible to go into every detail in this book, this chapter tried to get you in touch with the very powerful mathematical subroutines of ScaLAPACK by providing a typical example. To demonstrate one of ScaLAPACK's abilities, you were shown how to solve a positive definite tridiagonal symmetric linear equation system with the Cholesky factorization using ScaLAPACK's communication layer BLACS and two of ScaLAPACK's parallelizable math routines. The chapter ended by trying to give more insight into the underlying factorization method.

You saw that using these libraries is not quite straightforward and requires a lot of examples and exercises. It takes a lot of time to find useful documentations and apply these functions to specific problems. In the next two chapters, we will see that there are higher-level libraries that simplify these problems. Higher functions for solving linear and even nonlinear equation systems will enable you to use the full power of ScaLAPACK without caring too much about its complicated setup procedures, internal structures, and function calls.

# 5
# Advanced Solving of General Equation Systems

In the previous chapter, you were introduced to the ScaLAPACK library, which can be used to solve linear equation systems parallel to the distributed memory architecture. However, as you might have noticed, it is not an easy task to set up all the data structures that are required. First, it was necessary to plan a node grid that can be used for computations, and on this logical grid, calculation data has to be distributed correctly. A lot of experience and knowledge is required to perform such a task. Hence, it is not straightforward to program software that solves linear equations on your BeagleBone Black Cluster.

However, there are better options. In this chapter, we get to know the PETSc and SLEPc libraries, which are highly sophisticated and built upon ScaLAPACK and OpenMPI. With PETSc, it will become much easier to perform calculations such as solving linear, nonlinear, and even differential equation systems. SLEPc itself is a library that even enhances PETSc further and provides the functionality that solves Eigenvalue problems.

PETSc is well documented and has been developed since the 1990s. It will be developed and supported for many years in the future. A lot of scientific projects are built around this software library. Its applications include, but are not limited to, the following:

- Nano simulations
- Biology
- Plasma physics
- Geosciences
- Medicine
- Acoustics

All these different areas require solutions of linear, nonlinear, and Eigenvalue equations, which can be accomplished with PETSc and SLEPc. This chapter will start with the installation of PETSc. It will show you how to download, configure, and compile it on your BeagleBone Black cluster. It will continue with introducing you to the internal components of PETSc and its data types by explaining crucial examples. The chapter will then show you how to obtain, configure, and compile the SLEPc library, which builds upon PETSc. Some examples will show you how to solve linear, nonlinear, and Eigenvalue problems on your cluster. Let's first start with PETSc.

# PETSc – a toolkit for scientific computation

PETSc stands for portable, extensible toolkit for scientific computation. It provides its functionality on a higher level than ScaLAPACK and thus makes it easier to use for beginners. Furthermore, it is developed for use with C++, so there are no function name issues compared to porting the FORTRAN libraries of ScaLAPACK, such as the underscores we encountered in the previous chapter. The following figure shows you the internal components of the PETSc library:

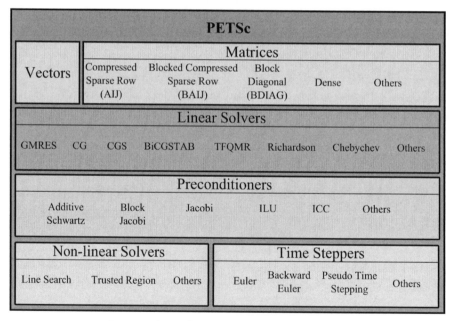

Important internal components of the PETSc library

Compared to handling vectors, which are not so critical, the proper storage of matrices can save a lot of memory and computation time. Mathematical problems often deal with special matrices that only have nonvanishing components in or near its diagonal. This leads to the idea to only save those diagonal or near-diagonal values that lead to the so-called sparse matrices. Sparse matrices, thus, are matrices where most of the components are zero. The compressed sparse row (AIJ) and blocked compressed sparse row (BAIJ) formats are used to save memory for sparse matrices. The opposite of sparse matrices is dense matrices, where most of the components are nonzero. They are usually saved in the used manner: number after number. The following figure shows you a generic example of a symmetric sparse matrix, where only the black blocks describe numbers that are nonzero. You probably noticed that there are lots of nonzero values far away from its diagonal. However, these matrices can be transformed so that all elements move closer to it. PETSc is able to store those matrices in an efficient manner.

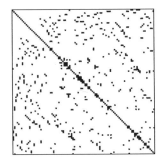

An example of a sparse matrix

While vector- and matrix-handling components provide storage for mathematical data, the other parts of PETSc deal with solving equations or systems of equations.

There are linear solvers that simplify and enhance the ScaLAPACK functionality. Linear solvers such as **Generalized Minimal Residual (GMRES)**, **Conjugate Gradients (CG)**, **Conjugate Gradients Squared (CGS)**, **BiConjugate Gradient Stabilized (BiCGSTAB)**, and **Transpose-Free Quasi-Minimal Residual (TFQMR)** are all based on the **Krylov** subspace. This means that they are based on iterations in the so-called Krylov subspace and are used for linear problems. The Krylov subspace was invented by Alexei Krylov in 1931 and uses matrix-vector multiplications instead of matrix-matrix multiplications. Methods based on this space can thus be used to speed up calculations on large sparse matrices and are among the most successful methods that are currently available in numerical linear algebra. For more details, you are encouraged to have a look at corresponding mathematics or numerical algorithm books, for example, *Numerical Linear Algebra, Lloyd N. Trefethen and David Bau, III, Society for Industrial and Applied Mathematics*.

The nonlinear solvers consist of well-known Newton-based methods such as **Line Search** and **Trusted Region**. The first method tries to find a local minimum using the local derivative, and the second method calculates an approximated function within a small interval in which it resembles the original function well. This region is then called the trusted region.

These two methods can be thought of as being dual. Line Search first calculates the step direction and then determines the step size, whereas Trusted Region first chooses a step size, and then calculates the step direction.

Time-steppers have the task of evolving time-dependent equation systems in time. The particular problem in this task is the stability of the system. Every time a system is evolved by a small step, the used method has to guarantee that the corresponding numerical error remains below a certain limit. For example, if you want to calculate the dynamics of a mass flow, numerical errors in time development can lead to a suddenly growing mass and therefore lead to wrong or even physically impossible results.

The last important component group contains the preconditioners. These are used to transform the input of the solver in order to reduce the error in the results and increase the numerical stability.

# Installing graphical libraries

Before we continue with configuring the compilation of PETSc, you should install the Xorg graphics system along with some development libraries. With these, we can add the graphical functionality to PETSc, and we will take a quick look at this in the next chapter. You can install everything by typing the following commands:

```
sudo apt-get install xorg
```

```
sudo apt-get install mesa-common-dev libgl1-mesa-dev libxt-dev libosmesa-
dev vtk
```

# Downloading and configuring PETSc

PETSc 3.3 worked on the PC but not on BBB. Version 3.4.1 worked and is used in this book. You can obtain this version at http://ftp.mcs.anl.gov/pub/petsc/release-snapshots/petsc-3.4.1.tar.gz.

Once you have downloaded this file to your MPI share directory, unpack it to a simple folder such as /var/mpishare/petsc, which is used in this book.

Before you can use the PETSc software library, you have to compile it from its source code. You have already installed BLACS, BLAS, and LAPACK along with ScaLAPACK; however, it is simpler to let the configuration script of PETSc download and compile these sources again, according to its needs. This will take the configuration script approximately 45 minutes to finish.

You can start the configuration with the following command from your `/var/mpishare/petsc-3.4.1` directory:

```
./configure --with-debugging=0 --download-f-blas-lapack
--download-scalapack --download-superlu
--download-superlu_dist PETSC_ARCH=arm-shared
--download-blacs --with-shared-libraries=1 --with-x
--download-metis --download-parmetis
--download-sowing
```

Let's first have a look at the meaning of all these parameters. Most sophisticated software libraries for calculations or similar purposes provide two modes that they can be compiled with. The first mode is the debugging mode, which enables additional error search possibilities if something is not working. However, debugging is a very hard job and requires a lot of experience to track errors down. Also, if you have tracked down an error, you have to correct it somehow. As this is above the abilities of most users and only possible for the inventors of the corresponding software libraries, compiling in the debug mode will only cause libraries to become slower and larger. To avoid this, we decide to compile it in the release mode or optimized mode. In this mode, PETSc can execute its calculations much faster. This is done with the following option:

```
--with-debugging=0
```

As mentioned previously, you have already installed the ScaLAPACK, BLAS, BLACS, and other libraries. However, there are different interface possibilities and a lot of different configuration parameters. To figure them all out, it might take you weeks or months. Also, compiling large software libraries such as PETSc on your BeagleBone Black cluster takes quite some time. To simplify things and avoid searching for errors because of wrongly configured libraries, let's tell the configure script or PETSc to download its mathematical base libraries again by itself and configure and compile it according to its own needs. We can do this using the following parameters:

```
--download-f-blas-lapack
--download-scalapack
--download-blacs
```

There are also different linear solvers that can perform a fast LU factorization of matrices. These are used by many sophisticated libraries built upon PETSc. To activate them, we tell the configure script to download the `superlu` and `superlu_dist` packages. The latter provides support for distributed memory applications such as parallel computation on our BeagleBone Black cluster:

`--download-superlu`

`--download-superlu_dist`

 Please pay attention to the underscore. This is `superlu_dist` and not `superlu-dist`, which would just ignore the option and continue without the SuperLU solver.

A very practical thing is to specify the PETSc architecture's name. With this name, you can compile and configure several different versions of PETSc and keep them separated cleanly. Later on, when we decide to compile another software package that is based on PETSc, we can specify this architecture name and use differently compiled PETSc libraries in the same system without getting confused or mixing up the system libraries. In my case, I have named the architecture `arm-shared`, which is done with the following parameter:

`PETSC_ARCH=arm-shared`

As this parameter already suggests, we are going to compile the PETSc library as a dynamically shared library. This is not because PETSc is too large, as it only has around 8 MB. However, imagine you build several small test applications with a few lines of code and link them with a static PETSc library; then, all of these programs will require this minimum size and take several MB storage space, although the actual program might only have a few KB in size. To avoid this, we will link our PETSc libraries dynamically. Furthermore, it is necessary to compile it with SLEPc and later the deal.II library, which we will handle in the next chapter. Building a shared library can be accomplished with the following configuration option:

`--with-shared-libraries=1`

PETSc also provides nice graphical output for a basic matrix display or other tasks. These routines are compatible with the Linux X window system. Later in this chapter, I will show you how to set up an X server on a Windows machine and forward access from your BeagleBone Black cluster to your Windows machine to enable the graphics output. In order to enable this feature in PETSc, you have to add the following configuration option:

`--with-x`

For more complex tasks, PETSc can be used on meshes, which describe real-world problems in the finite element formalism. For this purpose, PETSc supports different libraries that partition finite element meshes and the corresponding matrix optimizations. One library for this tasks that can be used is **Metis**, which is a software package from the University of Minnesota. The word means wisdom in Greek. The parallelized version of Metis is called **PARMetis**. PARMetis is also required by `superlu_dist`. To enable support for these important packages, we specify the following configuration parameter:

```
--download-metis
--download-parmetis
```

The last library, named `sowing`, is required for some FORTRAN compatibility issues and is required by the `SLEPc` library that we will deal with later in this chapter. It is activated with the following parameter:

```
--download-sowing
```

> The configuration process already compiles additional packages such as Metis, PARMetis, and SuperLU_DIST.

# Compiling PETSc

After the configuration script runs successfully, you can start compiling the PETSc library. To do this, just type the following command:

```
make PETSC_DIR=/var/mpishare/petsc-3.4.1 PETSC_ARCH=arm-shared all
```

This command automatically uses the generated makefile that was created by the configuration script in order to compile all the modules of PETSc and link them together into a dynamic shared library. The compilation will require approximately 89 minutes. This also depends on how many nodes you have installed with a working OpenMPI, as some parts of the build process run in parallel.

At the end of the compilation process, you might notice the following warning:

```
clock skew detected.
```

This means that some files have a time stamp that lies in the future. This is possible because PETSc tries to compile on several cluster nodes in parallel. When some of the cluster nodes have different time settings, freshly compiled object files can differ in their creation time. So, this is nothing to worry about.

When everything works out well, the dynamic library file will be created, which will have the full name: `/var/mpishare/petsc-3.4.1/arm-shared/lib/libpetsc.so`.

# Installing PETSc on your cluster nodes

To run parallel software based on this library, we have to tell every node where to locate this library file. However, there is a possibility to integrate the library file into the default search directories of the Linux operating system without using much additional memory. For this, just create a symbolic link on every node pointing to the common network share. Just type the following command on all your nodes:

```
sudo ln -s /var/mpishare/petsc-3.4.1/arm-shared/lib/libpetsc.so
usr/lib
```

This will create a symbolic link in `/usr/lib` and the program instances can run on all your cluster nodes using the same shared library file.

# PETSc example programs

To understand PETSc, let's first start with a very simple example: a typical "Hello World!" program. Create a folder in your network share named `petsctest` and create a file named `test1.cpp` with the following content:

```cpp
#include <petsc.h>

int main(int argc, char* argv[])
{
    PetscInitialize(&argc, &argv, PETSC_NULL, PETSC_NULL);
    PetscPrintf(PETSC_COMM_WORLD, "Hello World\n");
    PetscFinalize();
    return 0;
}
```

The first line includes the PETSc headers for function and constant definitions. The main function is defined in the usual C++ fashion with `argc` and `argv` parameters.

The first function call to `PetscInitialize` initializes the PETSc system according to any program parameters specified. Also included in this process is the initialization of OpenMPI.

A very interesting command is `PetscPrintf`. It is analogous to the C function `printf`, or the usage of the `std::cout` stream in C++; however, it only outputs the operand once, according to the `PETSC_COMM_WORLD` communicator. This communicator is based on the MPI communicator, `MPI_COMM_WORLD`, and is used to organize data between the cluster nodes. It is possible to run the PETSc system on a subset of the processes specified by `mpiexec`.

However, you have to create a corresponding communicator accordingly, before calling `PetscInitialize`. You can refer to the PETSc user manual for this: `http://www.mcs.anl.gov/petsc/petsc-current/docs/manualpages/Sys/PetscInitialize.html`.

Finally, the call to `PetscFinalize` tells PETSc that all process instances are about to quit and PETSc can free its internal memory allocations and other previously occupied resources. The example program will then return with exit code 0 according to the `return 0;` instruction.

# Compiling and running PETSc programs

To compile the previous example program, go to the source code directory and type the following:

```
mpic++ test1.cpp -I/var/mpishare/petsc-3.4.1/include
 -I/var/mpishare/petsc-3.4.1/arm-shared/include
 -L/var/mpishare/petsc-3.4.1/arm-shared/lib -lpetsc -o test1.out
```

This will specify `include` and the library directories with the `-I` and `-L` option respectively and link to the dynamic library `petsc`, as specified in the linker with the `-l` option. Do not type the `.so` extension when specifying a shared library file to the linker. The output file is specified to be `test1.out`.

When you created the symbolic link to `libpetsc.so` in `/usr/lib`, you don't need the `-L` option. After having successfully compiled example one, we can start it by typing the following:

```
mpirun -n 2 ./test1.out
```

It will produce the following output:

```
Hello World
```

# Simple vector math

PETSc is not only responsible for solving complicated equation systems, but it is also a complete user interface for linear and nonlinear problems, including differential equation systems, which also includes standard linear algebra. The main advantage of the direct ScaLAPACK interfacing is its simplicity. The following example program will show you how to calculate the norm of a vector, which means its length in $n$ dimensions. It will also show you how to use program parameters with PETSc and how to set vector elements that are distributed over several processes in your cluster.

Consider the following code in the `test2.cpp` file:

```
#include <math.h>
#include <petsc.h>
#include <petscvec.h>

int main(int argc, char* argv[])
{
    int rank;
    Vec x;
    int n = 20, ierr;
    PetscScalar one = 1.0, dot;

    PetscInitialize(&argc, &argv, PETSC_NULL, PETSC_NULL);
    PetscOptionsGetInt(PETSC_NULL, "--with-dimension", &n, PETSC_
NULL);
    MPI_Comm_rank(PETSC_COMM_WORLD, &rank);

    VecCreate(PETSC_COMM_WORLD, &x);
    VecSetSizes(x, PETSC_DECIDE, n);
    VecSetFromOptions(x);
    for (int i = 0; i < n; i++) {
        VecSetValue(x, (PetscInt) i, one, INSERT_VALUES);
    }
    VecDot(x, x, &dot);
    PetscPrintf(PETSC_COMM_WORLD, "Vector length: %f \n", sqrt(dot));
    VecDestroy(&x);

    PetscFinalize();

    return 0;
}
```

The preceding example includes `petscvec.h`, which includes definitions for vectors and vector operations. The variable rank is defined to obtain the process rank analogous to the OpenMPI samples. It is not used in this program. Notice the `PetscScalar` data type, which defines a number in the PETSc system. This is an abstract data type and depends on the configuration parameters of PETSc.

We could also have compiled PETSc for use with complex numbers directly. This would make PetscScalar equivalent to the C99 complex data type. However, this would produce issues with the deal.II library in *Chapter 6, Scientific and Technological Examples of Parallel Computing.*

We use this number to set the **vector** elements to 1.0. After the initialization of the PETSc system, the function call to PetscOptionsGetInt is used to obtain the command-line parameter value specified by --with-dimension. This value is then used to specify the dimensionality of the created vector. You can see that it is quite simple to use command-line parameters with this function. If the user does not specify such a parameter on starting the program, it is a good idea to initialize the variable with a standard value, which is 20 in our case. The next step is to create a vector. A vector is not just an array, because PETSc uses PBLAS and BLACS to manage data arrays with OpenMPI calls. You can think of a better PETSc vector to be a handle to some data structure internally managed by PETSc. However, as this is the case, you cannot just access different elements using array brackets such as v[i] = 1.0.

You have to use PETSc functions such as VecSetValue or VecSetValues for this purpose. First, the vector $x$ is created with the VecCreate command. This function also requires the PETSc communicator again in order to provide all the required parallelization possibilities. The VecSetSizes function manages the distribution of the vector onto the cluster nodes. The last parameter gives you the total number of vector dimensions. In our case, it has n dimensions, as specified by the --with-dimension program parameter. VecSetFromOptions is the last call for the vector creation. It sets vector properties according to the PETSc database from command-line options that can be set on the program execution. It belongs to the standard setup protocol and should not be omitted.

In the next program section, the vector elements are set by calling the VecSetValue function. The i parameter specifies the global element number of the vector.

Using VecSetValue with all the vector elements in this example will cause all instances on all cluster nodes to set the whole vector. This is inefficient and just intended to give an example.

Finally, the VecDot function performs a scalar product of the vector with itself. This retrieves the squared length of the vector, which is stored in the dot variable, which is a PetscScalar. Finally, the vector length is output by the PetscPrintf function as the square root of dot.

We compile the example with the following:

```
mpic++ test2.cpp -I/var/mpishare/petsc-3.4.1/include
    -I/var/mpishare/petsc-3.4.1/arm-shared/include -lpetsc -o test2.out
```

After this, we can start it with the following command:

```
mpiexec -n 2 ./test2.out --with-dimension 6
```

This will produce the following output:

```
Vector length: 2.449490.
```

This is the square root of six and thus gives you the length of a vector in six dimensions that have all elements set to one. For this run, two MPI processes were used as specified by the n parameter.

# Solving linear equations with SuperLU_DIST

You can find a lot of useful examples on solving linear equations at `http://www.mcs.anl.gov/petsc/petsc-current/src/ksp/ksp/examples/tutorials/index.html`.

However, you might be required to change small parts of the example code. I had to modify example 52 in order to compile it without an error. There are some forums on the Internet that you can find when you search for a solution to any problem.

One of the most sophisticated solver packages is SuperLU. In the following program, I have corrected the faulty PETSc example 52 and modified it to run with the SuperLU_DIST library. The code is provided as sld.cpp. As the code is longer than previous examples, I will explain it step by step and not list the whole code at once.

The program is intended to show you the difference between the SuperLU_DIST direct solver and standard internal PETSc iteration algorithms:

```
/* Solve linear system with SuperLU_DIST direct solver
/* modified and corrected PETSc example #52 by Andreas J. Reichel
/* 2014/08/05 */
#include <petscksp.h>

#undef __FUNCT__
#define __FUNCT__ "main"
int main(int argc, char **args)
{
```

The following code defines the solution vector x, the right-hand side of the equation (RHS), and the exact solution vector u. To understand this, we must have a look at the purpose of the program. In order to demonstrate the SuperLU abilities, we have to be able to argue whether a solution is good or not. How we do this will become clearer soon:

```
Vec             x, b, u;      // calculated solution, RHS, exact
solution
Mat             A;            // linear system matrix
KSP             ksp;          // linear solver context
```

As you can see, `Vec` defines vectors and `Mat` defines matrices. `KSP` is an object that represents the scalable Krylov subspace solvers, which means all linear solvers of PETSc, including optional ones.

Now, we define a context in order to generate random numbers. This is done by creating a variable with the `PetscRandom` data type. This is followed by some working variables:

```
PetscRandom    rctx;         // random number generator context
PetscReal      norm;         // norm of solution error
PetscInt       i, j, Ii, J, Istart, Iend, m = 4, n = 3, its;
PetscErrorCode ierr;
PetscBool      flg;
PetscScalar    v;
```

Now, initialize the PETSc system using the following command:

```
PetscInitialize(&argc, &args, NULL, NULL);
```

In the next step, we create the system matrix A for the linear equation system. The matrix is created with `MatCreate`. It also holds information on the MPI processes via `PETSC_COMM_WORLD`.

The matrix will have m*n rows and m*n columns; thus, it has m*n*m*n elements. This size is set with `MatSetSizes`:

```
ierr = MatCreate(PETSC_COMM_WORLD, &A); CHKERRQ(ierr);
ierr = MatSetSizes(A, PETSC_DECIDE, PETSC_DECIDE, m*n, m*n);
CHKERRQ(ierr);
ierr = MatSetFromOptions(A); CHKERRQ(ierr);
```

PETsc automatically distributes matrix and vector data onto the cluster nodes. MPIAIJ stands for global and parallel data, whereas SeqAIJ stands for local and sequential data. Every process gets a chunk of sequential data out of the global data:

```
    ierr = MatMPIAIJSetPreallocation(A, 5, NULL, 5, NULL);
CHKERRQ(ierr);
    ierr = MatSeqAIJSetPreallocation(A, 5, NULL); CHKERRQ(ierr);
    ierr = MatSetUp(A); CHKERRQ(ierr);
```

The following loop sets the system matrix for the equation system. Every process only sets its own part of the matrix data. For this purpose, the process has to first find out which elements belong to it. This is done with a call to the `MatGetownershipRange` function. The loop itself looks very hard to understand. It sets the actual linear equation system by initializing the matrix elements. The only important thing to understand here is that `MatGetOwnershipRange` returns two linear indices to the matrix data. The `Istart` pointer will point to the beginning of the local data chunk and `Iend` will point to its end. However, with every matrix, we want a column and a row to address it in the usual way. We can easily get the row index i by dividing the linear index by the number of columns, n. The j column index can then be retrieved by subtracting the number of elements up to the current row from the linear index:

```
// Set system matrix elements (5-point stencil in parallel)
ierr = MatGetOwnershipRange(A, &Istart, &Iend); CHKERRQ(ierr);
for (Ii = Istart; Ii < Iend; Ii++) {
   v = -1.0; i = Ii/n; j = Ii - i*n;
```

Then, the code sets data in the 5-point stencil method, which means that together with every matrix element, its four adjacent members are set. These are at positions `Ii - n` (above), `Ii + n` (below), `Ii - 1` (left), and `Ii + 1` (right). The values themselves are -1 for the adjacent data points and 4 for the direct data point. Furthermore, notice that we have `m*n` columns and `m*n` rows rather than m rows and n columns. The setup matrix corresponds to the Laplacian operator in two dimensions, which just means the second derivative. Thus, we do not see the stencil stars in the matrix itself as the matrix would show distorted elements:

```
    if (i > 0)     { J = Ii - n; ierr = MatSetValues(A, 1, &Ii, 1, &J,
        &v, INSERT_VALUES); CHKERRQ(ierr); }
    if (i < m - 1) { J = Ii + n; ierr = MatSetValues(A, 1, &Ii, 1, &J,
        &v, INSERT_VALUES); CHKERRQ(ierr); }
    if (j > 0)     { J = Ii - 1; ierr = MatSetValues(A, 1, &Ii, 1, &J,
        &v, INSERT_VALUES); CHKERRQ(ierr); }
    if (j < n - 1) { J = Ii + 1; ierr = MatSetValues(A, 1, &Ii, 1, &J,
        &v, INSERT_VALUES); CHKERRQ(ierr); }
    v = 4.0; ierr = MatSetValues(A, 1, &Ii, 1, &Ii, &v, INSERT_
                                VALUES); CHKERRQ(ierr);
}
```

We only saw how to assemble a matrix properly in a shared memory model, but we also saw that a two-dimensional problem can be formulated by a one-dimensional equation system.

The following commands assemble the actual matrix from all the MPI data and tells PETSc to perform all additional internal setup required:

```
// Assemble matrix using the 2-step process
ierr = MatAssemblyBegin(A, MAT_FINAL_ASSEMBLY); CHKERRQ(ierr);
ierr = MatAssemblyEnd(A, MAT_FINAL_ASSEMBLY); CHKERRQ(ierr);
```

Between these two commands, we can also perform some other calculations. With the following command, we tell PETSc that our matrix is symmetric. The reason is obvious. As with a symmetric matrix, the upper and the lower parts are identical, and we can save half of the storage memory and accelerate solvers:

```
// A is symmetric. Set symmetric flag to enable ICC/Cholesky
preconditioner
ierr = MatSetOption(A, MAT_SYMMETRIC, PETSC_TRUE);CHKERRQ(ierr);
```

Now, we create a parallelized vector u, which has m*n rows, and we duplicate it twice to get additional vectors b and x:

```
// Create the parallel MPIaij vectors
ierr = VecCreate(PETSC_COMM_WORLD, &u); CHKERRQ(ierr);
ierr = VecSetSizes(u, PETSC_DECIDE, m*n); CHKERRQ(ierr);
ierr = VecSetFromOptions(u); CHKERRQ(ierr);
ierr = VecDuplicate(u, &b); CHKERRQ(ierr);
ierr = VecDuplicate(b, &x); CHKERRQ(ierr);
```

Now, the trick is to provide the solution that we want to calculate. So, we already know the solution and we can compare it later with the calculated result to check whether it's correct. To make things more interesting, we set the vector components to random values. This is done with the PETSc random number generator:

```
// Set exact solution vector x to random values; then compute right-
hand-side vector b.

ierr = PetscRandomCreate(PETSC_COMM_WORLD, &rctx);CHKERRQ(ierr);
ierr = PetscRandomSetFromOptions(rctx); CHKERRQ(ierr);
ierr = VecSetRandom(u, rctx); CHKERRQ(ierr);
ierr = PetscRandomDestroy(&rctx); CHKERRQ(ierr);
```

Now, we can multiply the system matrix A to calculate the RHS of the equation. Afterwards, we pretend that u is unknown and solve the generated linear problem:

```
ierr = MatMult(A,u,b); CHKERRQ(ierr);
```

Furthermore, let's define a program option called `-view_exact_sol`. If you specify it on the program run, then the original vector u and the solution vector x will be printed out:

```
// View the exact solution vector if desired
flg  = PETSC_FALSE;
ierr = PetscOptionsGetBool(NULL, "-view_exact_sol", &flg, NULL);
CHKERRQ(ierr);
```

This can be achieved by the `VecView` function. There is also a `MatView` function that prints out matrices:

```
if (flg) { ierr = VecView(u, PETSC_VIEWER_STDOUT_WORLD);
CHKERRQ(ierr); }

// Create linear solver context
```

Calling `KSPCreate` will create our actual solver context. The solver context will be responsible for solving the linear equation:

```
ierr = KSPCreate(PETSC_COMM_WORLD,&ksp); CHKERRQ(ierr);
```

`KSPSetOperators` sets the system matrix (first A) and the matrix for the preconditioner (second A), which are the same in our example. The preconditioner is responsible for transforming the problem into a suitable form for a numerical solution:

```
ierr = KSPSetOperators(ksp,A,A,SAME_NONZERO_PATTERN); CHKERRQ(ierr);
```

The following code is just compiled if PETSc has built-in SUPERLU_DIST features. If you have compiled the library according to this book, it will be enabled so that the following code is compiled:

```
#if defined(PETSC_HAVE_SUPERLU_DIST)
  PetscPrintf(PETSC_COMM_WORLD, "superlu_dist defined\n");

  flg = PETSC_FALSE;
  ierr = PetscOptionsGetBool(NULL, "-use_superlu_dist", &flg, NULL);
CHKERRQ(ierr);
  if (flg) {
    ierr = KSPSetType(ksp, KSPPREONLY); CHKERRQ(ierr);
    PC pc;
    Mat F;
```

```
    ierr = KSPGetPC(ksp, &pc); CHKERRQ(ierr);
    ierr = PCSetType(pc, PCLU); CHKERRQ(ierr);
    ierr = PCFactorSetMatSolverPackage(pc, MATSOLVERSUPERLU_DIST);
CHKERRQ(ierr);
    ierr = PCFactorSetUpMatSolverPackage(pc); CHKERRQ(ierr);
    ierr = PCFactorGetMatrix(pc, &F); CHKERRQ(ierr);
  }
#endif
```

The whole trick to use SuperLU_DIST instead of internal PETSc solvers is to set properties of the KSP solver context. For this, there are four important functions as follows::

- KSPSetType: This builds the context according to the solver type
- KSPGetPC: This gets the preconditioner's context
- PCSetType: This sets the preconditioner's type
- PCFactorSetMatSolverPackage: This sets the factorization software package

The KSP type is set to KSPPREONLY, which is correct for SuperLU. The preconditioner is set to LU factorization by specifying PCLU to PCSetType. Then, the SuperLU_DIST software package is selected by a call to PCFactorSetMatSolverPackage:

```
ierr = KSPSetFromOptions(ksp); CHKERRQ(ierr);
//     Get info from matrix factors
ierr = KSPSetUp(ksp); CHKERRQ(ierr);
```

After setting up the solver context, we can finally solve the equation system with KSPSolve. The first parameter is the solver context, the second parameter is the RHS, and the third parameter is the handle of the unknown vector x:

```
//     Solve the linear system
ierr = KSPSolve(ksp,b,x); CHKERRQ(ierr);
```

If you pass the program option to view the vectors, the following code is responsible for doing so:

```
flg  = PETSC_FALSE;
 ierr = PetscOptionsGetBool(NULL, "-view_exact_sol", &flg,NULL);
CHKERRQ(ierr);
```

It will first output the calculated vector, x, to the console:

```
 if (flg) {ierr = VecView(x, PETSC_VIEWER_STDOUT_WORLD);
CHKERRQ(ierr);}
```

The `VecAXPY` function computes alpha times x plus y. In our case, this leads to x = u - x, which defines the difference between the computed and given solution, namely the error vector:

```
//     Check solution and clean up
ierr = VecAXPY(x, -1.0, u); CHKERRQ(ierr);
```

Finally, we get the length of the error vector that is defined by the 2-norm (the square root norm). This is used as a quality criterion for our solution:

```
ierr = VecNorm(x, NORM_2, &norm); CHKERRQ(ierr);
```

We can also retrieve the number of iterations used by the solver:

```
ierr = KSPGetIterationNumber(ksp, &its); CHKERRQ(ierr);
```

Now, print out this information, release the memory, and end the program:

```
//     Print convergence information
ierr = PetscPrintf(PETSC_COMM_WORLD, "Norm of error: %g, iterations:
%D\n", (double)norm, its); CHKERRQ(ierr);

//  Free work space
ierr = KSPDestroy(&ksp); CHKERRQ(ierr);
ierr = VecDestroy(&u);   CHKERRQ(ierr);
ierr = VecDestroy(&x);   CHKERRQ(ierr);
ierr = VecDestroy(&b);   CHKERRQ(ierr);
ierr = MatDestroy(&A);   CHKERRQ(ierr);

ierr = PetscFinalize();
return 0;
}
```

# Direct solvers versus iterative solvers

Now, we can run the previously explained example program after compiling it with the following command:

```
mpic++ sld.cpp -I/var/mpishare/petsc-3.4.1/arm-shared/include
  -I/var/mpishare/petsc-3.4.1/include -lpetsc -o sld
```

We have two possibilities in order to run it. First, we will run it with the usual internal PETSc linear solvers on four processes by typing the following:

```
mpirun -n 4 ./sld -view_exact_sol
```

The output should be as follows:

```
Vector Object: 4 MPI processes
  type: mpi
Process [0]
0.720032
0.061794
0.0100223
Process [1]
0.54...
1144
```

You can now compare the output above the superlu_dist-defined line, and there should be a difference of 0.000001 between the first components.

The output ends with the following:

```
Norm of error: 6.44807e-06, iterations: 9
```

This indicates that the solver requires nine iterative steps to find a good solution. The error is in the order of 1E6.

Now, we can test the program with the SuperLU_DIST solver. To do this, start the program with the following command:

```
mpirun -n 4  ./sld -use_superlu_dist -view_exact_sol
```

You will now see that both output parts are identical and that the output ends with the following:

```
Norm of error: 1.24127e-16, iterations: 1
```

This means that the SuperLU_DIST solver only requires one iteration instead of nine, and the solution is more precise by a factor of 1E10. This is the case because SuperLU is a direct solver, whereas previously, we ran an iterative solver.

# Solving nonlinear equations with SNES

SNES stands for Scalable Nonlinear Equation Solver. As we have solved linear equations in the previous chapters, we will now deal with another type of equations: nonlinear equations. The main difference is that they cannot be described by a linear system matrix, of course. Instead, we must have a function that is evaluated in our software.

Furthermore, we need derivatives of our function that are evaluated on specific locations. To understand how the concept of solving nonlinear equation systems works, you can have a look at the `snes.cpp` example. It is taken from example 5 of the PETSc SNES tutorials. For more information about this program, please visit www.mcs.anl.gov/petsc/petsc-3.4/src/snes/examples/tutorials/ex5.c.html.

In this section, I will only discuss the main differences between solving nonlinear equations with SNES and solving linear equations with KSP.

The problem solved with this program is given in the form $-\Delta u(x,y) - \lambda e^{u(x,y)} = 0$ in the area $0 < x,y < 1$ with the condition that `u(x,y)` is zero around the boundaries $x = 0, y = 0, x = 1 \text{ or } y = 1$.

This is a nonlinear differential equation system of the second order, as it contains the second derivatives of u in the Laplace operator on the left-hand side. The parameter $\lambda$ defines the size of the nonlinearity.

This equation is called the Bratu equation and it is used in but is not limited to:

- Solid fuel ignition models
- Heat transfer via radiation
- Nanotechnology
- Cosmology

Let's have a look at the program's logic.

First, a solver context is created, which is similar to the KSP we used before. This is done by calling `SNESCreate`.

One new thing is the use of distributed arrays. These distributed arrays are able to treat parallel vectors and grids. A grid defines the partitioning of the space we solve the equation with. The DMDA-functions deal with the grid creation and incorporates vector maths. On every recursion, the grid is automatically coarsened or refined where required. The `DMDACreate2d` function creates a two-dimensional geometric grid and distributes it on the MPI processes. After the creation, uniform coordinates are set and the grid is connected to the SNES solver. Vectors for the calculations have to be of global DM type. This means that they are created with `DMCreateGlobalVector`.

A very important part of the program is the DMDASNESSetFunctionLocal function, which sets the local form function for the SNES solver. The local form function is nothing else but the numerical evaluation of our nonlinear function. In the example file, it sets the form function to FormFunctionLocal, which you can find below the main program. At the very end of this function, you will find this line:

```
f[j][i] = uxx + uyy - sc*PetscExpScalar(u);
```

Here, uxx and uyy are the discrete second derivatives of the unknown u function on the grid regarding the x and y coordinates, respectively. The sc variable holds our lambda parameter, which is adapted to the discrete grid, whereas PetscExpScalar evaluates the exponential function.

After setting our nonlinear function for the solver, we have to take an initial guess. This is required because the solver needs a starting point from which it will walk away and look at what happens to the equation. The direction and step size is then adapted until a good enough solution is found. The guess is provided by the call to FormInitialGuess. It gets the vector data from PETSc by calling DMDAVecGetArray, sets the values of the guessed solution, and releases the vector by calling DMDAVecRestoreArray.

The final step is to call SNESSolve in order to get the final solution vector, which is x.

For simplicity, only the required parts of the program were kept, and I deleted all the advanced stuff because it is not possible to explore everything in this book. If you are interested, you can refer to the PETSc user manual at www.mcs.anl.gov/petsc/petsc-current/docs/manual.pdf.

Run the program, and it will output the used number of iterations in order to find a solution.

# SLEPc – a library for Eigenvalue problems

SLEPc stands for Scalable Library for Eigenvalue Problem Computations. With this library, it is possible to solve Eigenvalues and Eigenvectors. These problems are infamous in quantum mechanics. Before we go a little into details, we will download, configure, and compile the SLEPc extension library.

# Downloading and configuring SLEPc

Download Version 3.4.4 from `http://www.grycap.upv.es/slepc/download/download.htm`.

 SLEPc and PETSc must match in their main and first subversions. So, 3.4.4 and 3.4.1 are fine, and 3.5 and 3.1 will probably not work.

To install SLEPc, extract the archive with the following command:

```
tar -xf petsc-3.4.4.tar.gz
```

Go to the `petsc-3.4.4` subdirectory and type the following:

```
export PETSC_DIR=/var/mpishare/petsc-3.4.1
export PETSC_ARCH=arm-shared
export SLEPC_DIR=/var/mpishare/slepc-3.4.4
./configure
```

This takes only a minute.

 In order to install SLEPc, PETSc must already be compiled!

The configure script will finish with the following output:

```
xxx===========================================================xxx
 Configure stage complete. Now build the SLEPc library with (cmake
build):
   make SLEPC_DIR=$PWD PETSC_DIR=/var/mpishare/petsc-3.4.1 PETSC_
ARCH=arm-shared
xxx===========================================================xxx
```

# Compiling SLEPc

According to the output of the configure script, type the following command to compile SLEPc:

```
make SLEPC_DIR=$PWD PETSC_DIR=/var/mpishare/petsc-3.4.1
  PETSC_ARCH=arm-shared
```

On my cluster, the build script automatically used two processes that took 8 minutes to compile. Now, you can test whether everything is working by typing the following:

```
make test
```

This will only take around 18 seconds and should give you the following output:

```
Running test examples to verify correct installation
Using SLEPC_DIR=/var/mpishare/slepc-3.4.4, PETSC_DIR=/var/mpishare/
petsc-3.4.1 and PETSC_ARCH=arm-shared
C/C++ example src/eps/examples/tests/test10 run successfully with 1 MPI
process
C/C++ example src/eps/examples/tests/test10 run successfully with 2 MPI
process
Fortran example src/eps/examples/tests/test7f run successfully with 1 MPI
process
Completed test examples
```

As done previously with PETSc, create a symbolic link to the library in `/usr/lib` by executing the following command on all cluster nodes:

```
sudo ln -s /var/mpishare/slepc-3.4.4/arm-shared/lib/libslepc.so
  /usr/lib
```

# A SLEPc example program

Now, we are ready to solve the first Eigenvalue problem. A good demonstration is example 1, which is part of the slepc software. It demonstrates how to solve the equation.

$$Av = kv$$

Here, **A** is the one-dimensional Laplace operator and, in our case, **k** is the Eigenvalue. We will now explain the geometrical key idea of Eigenvalues.

Linear operators such as rotation matrices can rotate, but they can also elongate or mirror vectors if multiplied by them. A vector that is not rotated but just changed in its length is called an Eigenvector to this matrix. The scale factor is the Eigenvalue.

A very simple example we will see here is the analogy to a free particle problem in quantum mechanics. Here, the 1-D Laplace operator is the momentum operator, which represents the Hamiltonian (the energy of the system). Free particles only have kinetic energy but no potential energy (it can always be redefined to a constant zero), which is already given by the momentum operator. The Eigenvectors are then solutions that represent free particles.

Download the example from `http://www.grycap.upv.es/slepc/handson/` `handson1.html`. You can modify it and add `PetscTime` calls to measure the time it requires to get the solution. To do this, search the line that calls `EPSSolve(eps)`, and add the following lines surrounding this call:

```
PetscLogDouble t1, t2;

ierr = PetscTime(&t1);CHKERRQ(ierr);
ierr = EPSSolve(eps);CHKERRQ(ierr);
ierr = PetscTime(&t2);CHKERRQ(ierr);
ierr = PetscPrintf(PETSC_COMM_WORLD, "Solution took %f
  seconds.\n", t2-t1);CHKERRQ(ierr);
```

You also have added an `include` instruction for `petsctime.h` in the file header:

```
#include <petsctime.h>
```

## Compiling a SLEPc program

In order to compile a SLEPc program, you have to link it to both SLEPc and PETSc libraries. To do this, you can either specify the full library path to the compiler, or you can create symbolic links from the library files to /usr/lib, as shown earlier in this chapter. Then, the linker just needs the library names in order to find them. We assume that you have set these symbolic links, and then the full compile command is as follows:

```
mpic++ ex1.c -I/var/mpishare/petsc-3.4.1/include
 -I/var/mpishare/petsc-3.4.1/arm-shared/include
 -I/var/mpishare/slepc-3.4.4/include
 -I/var/mpishare/slepc-3.4.4/arm-shared/include -lslepc -lpetsc
 -o ex1
```

As you can see, the compiler requires all the paths to the PETSc and SLEPc include files. You can also write a makefile. Makefiles will be explained in the next chapter.

# Demonstrating the cluster's scaling ability

Run your previously compiled SLEPc program with the order of 256, which will create a matrix with 65,536 elements, by typing the following command:

```
mpirun -n 1 ./ex1 -n 256 -eps_max_it 100
```

The output will show you the first Eigenvalue and the relative calculation error:

```
1-D Laplacian Eigenproblem, n=256


Solution took 0.745027 seconds.
 Number of iterations of the method: 70
 Solution method: krylovschur


 Number of requested eigenvalues: 1
 Stopping condition: tol=1e-08, maxit=4096
 Number of converged eigenpairs: 1


        k                ||Ax-kx||/||kx||
---------------- ------------------
     3.999851        9.87003e-09
```

As you can see, the solution converged quickly after 0.7 seconds. Now you surely want to try the scaling abilities of the software and see whether this can be faster when using several nodes in parallel. Run the program again with the following command:

```
mpirun -n 4 ./ex1 -n 256 -eps_max_it 100
```

Don't be astonished if the result is the opposite of what you might have expected. In my tests, this took almost 5 times longer, namely 3.2 seconds to finish. So, why does the cluster not scale as we expected? This is the case simply because all the OpenMPI message passing and data distribution over the network and between the software components takes some time. If the data messaging takes longer than actual computations, we degrade the cluster's efficiency rather than scaling the calculation time down.

The following screenshot shows you some test results I gained with problem sizes from **n=256** to **n=4096**:

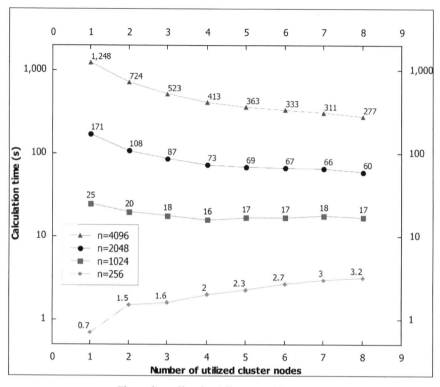

The scaling effect for different problem sizes

You can see that the scaling effect is clearly dominant for larger problem sizes. So, for every problem, there is a maximum amount of cluster nodes that should be utilized in order to get the optimum performance. For very huge problems in modern applications, such as simulating the origin of the universe, this does not play a role and calculations are always accelerated.

 In many numerical applications, refining a computation grid results in more exact solutions; however, it has to be ruled out if the calculation time and number of required solution iteration steps are in a reasonable ratio.

# Summary

In this chapter, you were introduced to the PETSc and SLEPc libraries. With PETSc, linear and nonlinear equations can be solved in a novel way. You were shown how to download and compile the PETSc library with the optional high-efficiency algorithm SuperLU for the distributed memory architecture. Also, some additional features were installed, which will play an important role in the following chapter.

Some simple PETSc examples explained how to treat parallel vectors and matrices and how each process can access its own and foreign parts. Starting with simple examples from calculating the vector norm in n-dimensions to solving a symmetric linear equation, you were shown how to use SuperLU to solve a two-dimensional Laplace equation. Using this example, you could also see the difference between a direct solver and an iterative solver.

Advancing the abilities of PETSc even further, we downloaded and configured the SLEPc library, which is a powerful software package that solves Eigenvalue problems, which are very common in all varieties of practical applications. As an example, we solved the first Eigenvalue of the discretized Laplace operator in a customizable grid spacing, which can be understood as the first solution for the quantum mechanical free particle problem.

With all these examples, you got to know the standard way to set up mathematical problems in PETSc and SLEPc, and you saw that it is easier than using BLACS and ScaLAPACK directly.

With the last example, you could also see the scaling abilities of your BeagleBone Black cluster. Huge problems can be scaled down in time, and this makes your self-built, low-cost super computer a highly sophisticated tool for many kinds of applications in practical or theoretical numerical simulations.

In the next chapter, we will see how to further improve these features with the `deal.II` library. With `deal.II`, a lot more possibilities for file handling, such as solution storage and visualization as well as interfacing with many well-established file formats, will be added to our super computer. We will see that although we already eased programming techniques with PETSc and SLEPc a lot, `deal.II` is more advanced regarding the dimensionality of problems and programming formalism. We will encounter and simulate many modern simulation examples and visualize solutions using modern, well-established file formats. In the following chapter, the full calculation power of our cluster will be utilized easily.

# 6
# Scientific and Technological Examples of Parallel Computing

In the last two chapters, you saw different examples of how to utilize the scalable computational power of your self-built BeagleBone Black cluster. You saw that special software libraries and some programming skills are necessary in order to create the required tools. In *Chapter 4*, *Parallel Computing with OpenMPI and ScaLAPACK*, you gained basic knowledge of how the calculation power is distributed using OpenMPI and how to utilize it to solve problems in linear algebra.

In *Chapter 5*, *Advanced Solving of General Equation Systems Using Advanced Methods*, you got to know about a much simpler approach for an even broader area of mathematical problems. With the two libraries SLEPc and PETSc, you saw how to solve linear, nonlinear, and Eigenvalue equations, which are very common in scientific and general technological questions but also appear in financial problems and many other areas.

In this chapter, you will get to know about a highly sophisticated library called **deal. II**, which has been developed at the Numerical Methods Group at the University of Heidelberg in Germany. It is available to create free and commercial software that solves very complex problems based on **finite** elements. What finite elements are will be explained shortly in this chapter. Mainly, the following topics will be covered:

- Key ideas behind finite elements
- Introduction to the deal.II library
- The configuration and compilation of the deal.II library
- Useful examples that show the basic usage and possibilities deal.II provides
- Easy but very powerful methods that visualize calculation results

# Calculations on cloud-distributed mesh grids

In order to distribute mathematical problems onto a cluster, it is necessary to create a logical plan that maps the data array onto the logical computation nodes. In technological or scientific calculations, a real body or space often builds the basis for a fundamental description. For example, we want to calculate the strain inside a two-dimensional body or the heat transfer from one side to the other side of this body. In order to do this, it is necessary to describe this body in a mathematical manner.

## The triangulation of a body mesh

To accomplish this description, you need to calculate all the physical properties of all infinitesimally small constituents of it. Usually, this would be atoms or molecules. However, a sugar cube already contains around 10 to the power of 21 atoms. These are thousands of billions of billions of atoms. If you want to store a few numbers, for example, eight double format floating point numbers for each of these atoms, you will need more than a few billion terabytes of memory.

From the previous examples in *Chapter 5, Advanced Solving of General Equation Systems using Advanced Methods*, you got an idea how long the solving of equation systems takes with such an unimaginable huge amount of unknowns. It would take longer than you are alive on modern hardware. Even if you succeed, you could never store the data. To solve this problem, the body is divided into a given amount of discrete parts. For example, we can define a set of points that describe the area or 2D-volume of our flat body. This set of points can then be connected by triangles. This is called triangulation. For the triangulation, a special rule applies, which is called the **Delaunay criterion**. This criterion states that the circumcircle of each triangle does not enclose any other additional point of the body but only has the three points on it that define the triangle.

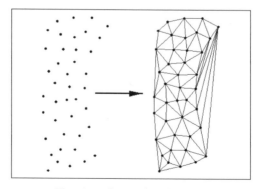

The triangulation of mesh points

Convenient methods exist inside the deal.II library, which will be introduced shortly in this chapter. With these methods, mesh grids can be triangulated and also automatically refined according to the problem's complexity.

# Finite elements

As we have now defined a two-dimensional set of triangles that define the surface of our body, we can apply mathematical equations to the triangles. These equations will then allow us to find an approximate solution for our problem. Of course, the elements of the body surface do not need to be triangles. They can also be rectangles or other differently shaped objects. It is only important that the whole area be divided into a subset of small areas. To understand the mathematical background, let's take a deeper look at the two-dimensional solution of a temperature gradient.

# A practical example – the temperature gradient

Let's consider a very practical problem: we look at the two-dimensional cross-section of a usual living room with a window, a heater below the window and a floor, a sidewall, as well as the ceiling. Now, we want to calculate the stationary temperature profile in this room. As a first step, we have to find the required equation that can describe the problem. This is done using the time-independent heat transfer equation, which reads as follows:

$$\Delta u(x, y) = 0$$

Here, **u** is the temperature profile, which is a function that has two coordinates. Additionally, this function might have different boundary conditions, which set its values on its boundaries, that is, on the walls of the room. Now, we divide the room into a discrete set of points. The easiest way is to use rectangles. Doing this, we will get a u[i,j] function, which means that we have a two-dimensional data array with two indices, where the first sets the position on the x-axis and j sets the position on the y-axis, which is a multiple of the decided grid point distance—h. The Laplace operator, which means the second derivative, must also be discretized to solve this problem numerically. This is done by replacing the infinitesimally small differentials by differences that approximate them. As known from analytical maths, it is possible to expand differentiable functions into polynomials using their differentials. One way to do this is using the Taylor expansion through which the temperature u[i+1,j] can be written using the u[i,j] temperature. This means that the right neighboring grid point is approximated by its left neighbor.

We can write this equation as follows:

$$u[i + 1, j] = u[i, j] + u'[i, j]h + \frac{1}{2}u''[i, j]h^2 + \cdots$$

Likewise, for the left neighbor point, we can write this equation:

$$u[i - 1, j] = u[i, j] - u'[i, j]h + \frac{1}{2}u''[i, j]h^2 + \cdots$$

These two equations yield the following result:

$$u''[i, j] = \frac{1}{h^2}(u[i + 1, j] - 2u[i, j] + u[i - 1, j]) + \cdots$$

Here, the dots always denote small amounts that can be neglected if the grid point distance h gets small enough. The two primes denote the second derivative in x, which can also be denoted in y, leading to the following:

$$u''[i, j] = \frac{1}{h^2}(u[i, j + 1] - 2u[i, j] + u[i, j - 1]) + \cdots$$

Adding these two differential approximations in x and y, we get the discretized Laplace operator as follows:

$$\Delta u[i, j] \approx \frac{1}{h^2}(u[i + 1, j] + u[i - 1, j] + u[i, j + 1] + u[i, j - 1] - 4u[i, j])$$

In general, the heat transfer problem can then be written as follows:

$$u[i + 1, j] + u[i - 1, j] + u[i, j + 1] + u[i, j - 1] - 4u[i, j] = h^2 f[i, j]$$

Here, f[i,j] was zero in our heat transport equation.

With a simple lexicographic rule, we can map the two dimensional data arrays u[i,j] and f[i,j] onto one-dimensional vectors using U[k] = u[i,j] with k = iN + j, where N is the number of grid points in x-direction. Likewise, we can define F[k] = f[i,j]. This leads to the following matrix equation:

$$AU = F$$

Here, **U** and **F** are the vectors given by the grid point values. The matrix **A** is then defined by the following block matrix:

$$A = \begin{pmatrix} A_0 & I & 0 & 0 & 0 \\ I & A_0 & I & 0 & 0 \\ 0 & \ddots & \ddots & \ddots & 0 \\ 0 & 0 & I & A_0 & I \\ 0 & 0 & 0 & I & A_0 \end{pmatrix}$$

Here, $I$ is the identity matrix and $A0$ is the discretized Laplace operator in matrix formalism, which means the following:

$$A_0 = \begin{pmatrix} -4 & 1 & 0 & 0 & 0 \\ 1 & -4 & 1 & 0 & 0 \\ 0 & \ddots & \ddots & \ddots & 0 \\ 0 & 0 & 1 & -4 & 1 \\ 0 & 0 & 0 & 1 & -4 \end{pmatrix}$$

These matrices can have different appearances depending on the method of the mesh generation. However, we have seen that the Laplace equation leads to a spare block matrix that consist of spare matrices. These systems can be solved efficiently.

Now that we have gained a very basic understanding of a two-dimensional finite element description of a heat transfer problem, we continue with the introduction of the deal.II library and how it can be used to treat such problems.

# deal.II – a powerful Physics calculation library

deal.II is a highly sophisticated simulation library based on the method of finite elements. It is developed by professional mathematicians and programmers, and it is open source software. The first question that might arise is why should you use the deal.II library at all. This can be answered with the same argument as the one used for the other software library we have already used. You can, of course, write everything yourself from scratch. However, you only have limited time each day to write your code, and also, you do not want to have just a simple algorithm for a specific problem. You probably want code that is state of the art and very efficient in problem solving. However, not many people would have the knowledge to write highly optimized code and this also takes a very long time. Again, it becomes very clear why deal.II is helpful. It is a complete library already optimized to run on cluster systems and solve different kinds of engineering or scientific problems.

What we want to be state of the art in general are the following:

- Adaptive meshes, which means that our mesh is refined with each solution iteration that provides more details where required but also keeps memory requirements as low as possible

- Quadratic or even higher order elements in order to get access to higher order solutions

- Multigrid solvers

- Scalability to thousands of processors, which have already been realized with PETSc and SLEPc

- Efficient use of current hardware, which depends on the message passing, in our case, OpenMPI

- Graphical output suitable for high quality rendering, which we will demonstrate using special file formats that allow us to use sophisticated visualization software later in this chapter

There is already an excellent software to solve such problems. For example, you can use the already discussed libraries, which are BLAS and LAPACK, from the previous chapters to solve linear problems on your cluster. Also, there is the PETSc library, which we used for parallel computations. Finally, the functionality for mesh handling and finite elements is realized on top of these libraries, and everything is combined in an easily manageable way in the deal.II software library.

# Obtaining deal.II

You can obtain the deal.II library from the Packt Publishing website (`http://www.packtpub.com`):

Please note that this is not the newest version. However, beginning from Version 8.0.0, you will need Version 2.8.8 or higher of the cmake development tool, which is not obtainable for our chosen operating system. In order to use a newer deal. II library, you will have to compile cmake yourself, which is not described in this book. Version 7.3.0 works well. Download and unpack this version into your `/var/mpishare` folder. This will create a folder named `/var/mpishare/deal.II`.

The source code already contains the optional linear solver **Unsymmetric MultiFrontal sparse LU factorization (UMFPACK)**. This enables robust direct solving if the linear system matrix is not symmetric.

As deal.II also builds upon low-level math libraries such as BLAS, the easiest way to correctly compile deal.II and derived applications is to install the standard Ubuntu BLAS in this case. For this, execute the following command on each node:

```
sudo apt-get install libblas-dev
```

# Configuring deal.II

The deal.II library will be configured to build upon our previously compiled PETSc and SLEPc libraries. Also, we will provide the METIS graph-partitioning library. This library will enable the efficient partitioning of a mesh onto the cluster nodes by minimizing the number of cut edges, which will reduce the amount of parallel network communication.

In order to configure deal.II correctly, you will need to perform a modification as described in the following information box:

There is a block of code lines that needs to be removed from the configuration program in order to successfully integrate PETSc 3.4.1 and SLEPc 3.4.4. Usually, deal.II wants exactly the same subversions of the libraries. To prevent this (major and minor revisions are fine), we can open the `/var/mpishare/deal.II/configure` file and search for the `if` statement that compares the two versions. You will find it at line 10,595:

```
if test "${PETSC_VERSION}" != "${SLEPC_VERSION}" \
-o "${PETSC_RELEASE}" != "${SLEPC_RELEASE}" \
; then
.as_fn_error $? "If SLEPc is used, you must use the
same version number as your PETSc Installation"
"$LINENO" 5
fi
```

This code line is enclosed by an `if` and a `fi` command. Delete everything in between and include `if` and `fi` before and after line 10,595.

Make sure that you have performed the modifications according to the preceding information box, and type the following commands in your SSH shell according to your needs:

```
export PETSC_DIR=/var/mpishare/petsc-3.4.1
export SLEPC_DIR=/var/mpishare/slepc-3.4.4
export PETSC_ARCH=arm-shared
export SLEPC_ARCH=arm-shared
export METIS_DIR=/var/mpishare/metis
```

Then, run the `configure` command, which will take about 2.5 minutes:

```
./configure --disable-threads --with-mpi --with-umfpack
--with-blas=blas CXX=mpicxx CC=mpicc FC=mpif77 FF=mpif90
--with-petsc=/var/mpishare/petsc-3.4.1/
--with-petsc-arch=arm-shared
--with-metis=/var/mpishare/metis/metis-5.1.0
--with-slepc=/var/mpishare/slepc-3.4.4
--with-slepc-arch=arm-shared
```

The meaning of each of the single parameters in the preceding code is as follows:

- To compile deal.II, we have to disable the threading functionality. Otherwise, it will look for multithreading support for the ARM CPU, which does not exist. This is done with the `--disable-threads` parameter.

- Also, we want to specify that deal.II is compiled using our OpenMPI message-passing interface. This is enabled with the `--with-mpi` option.

- The previously extracted deal.II comes with the UMFPACK source code, which you can enable by specifying `--with-umfpack`.

- Likewise, `--with-blas=blas` will enable the `blas` math library, which is a core module like the one in ScaLAPACK. This will use the default BLAS, which is available on most Linux systems and links against `libblas.so.3gf`. The file is obtained by installing the `libblas-dev` packet as described at the end of the previous subsection.

- The `CXX`, `CC`, `FC`, and `FF` parameters specify the OpenMPI compiler wrappers to be sure that everything is compiled correctly in order to use the OpenMPI-libraries.

- Finally, the following five parameters specify the optional add-on module paths and configuration names:

  - `--with-petsc=/var/mpishare/petsc-3.4.1/`
  - `--with-petsc-arch=arm-shared`
  - `--with-metis=/var/mpishare/metis/metis-5.1.0`
  - `--with-slepc=/var/mpishare/slepc-3.4.4`
  - `--with-slepc-arch=arm-shared`

# Building deal.II

If you have finished your deal.II configuration and just typed `make optimized` to build it; you will see that the C++ compiler returns an error while trying to compile the `numerics/data_out.cc` file.

This happens because we run out of memory on the BeagleBone Black node. This is the reason why we need the external microSD card in our master node. This additional virtual memory can easily be added by first creating a swap file on the root filesystem. For example, you can issue the following command to generate an initial swap file on the root folder:

```
sudo dd if=/dev/zero of=/swapfile bs=1M count=1024
```

This will generate a file with a size of one gigabyte and write its contents to zero (from the virtual `/dev/zero` device that only returns zeros). Next, you can activate the swap file by typing the following:

```
sudo swapon /swapfile
```

Finally, start the build process:

```
make optimized
```

 Please note that the full build process will take around 510 minutes on a BeagleBone Black board. Plan your time to do something else meanwhile.

The last step is to modify the access rights to the dynamic link library, as there was something wrong after I built it. Go to the `/var/mpishare/deal.II/lib` folder and alter the file rights to grant full access rights to owner and group as well as read and execute rights to everybody by typing the following:

```
chmod 775 libdeal_II.so.7.3.0
```

We again create symbolic links to the system library directory by typing the following:

```
sudo ln -s /var/mpishare/deal.II/lib/libdeal.II.so.7.3.0
  /usr/lib/libdeal_II.so.7.3.0
```

```
sudo ln -s /var/mpishare/deal.II/lib/libdeal_II.so
  /usr/lib/deal_II.so
```

Finally, you have installed your self-compiled deal.II library.

# Example programs

To understand the possibilities of deal.II, it's best that we have a look at some of the standard example files that come with the package. You will see the `/var/mpishare/deal.II/examples` folder in your source directory tree. Go there and enter the directory of the first example called `step-1`.

As you have seen in the previous chapters, it is a time-consuming action to always specify every single link library when compiling your programs. Also, when you have programs with more than one object file, compiling this way will soon get annoying and unmanageable. However, there is a far better way to generate software, namely using the so-called **makefiles**.

# Using makefiles

A makefile is nothing but a file that contains all the compiler and linker information. It is a special file that is processed by a program called make. This program can be understood to be a simple command interpreter that makes software creation more flexible and convenient.

If you open the /var/mpishare/deal.II/examples/step-1/Makefile file with, for example, the mcedit editor, you will see different target definitions, followed by a colon. Most common definitions are all and clean. When you type make all in the same directory as the makefile, then usually, the whole software described by the makefile will be compiled without the need to specify anything more. To revert to the clean source code state, deleting all previously compiled parts, you can usually type:

**make clean**

These two commands refer to the defined targets in the makefile. It is not possible to explain all the possibilities of the GNU make; however, there is a lot of information on the Internet if you just perform a search on Google.

# First deal.II example – triangulation

To start with the first deal.II example, go to the examples/step-1 folder in your deal.II source location. As we have compiled deal.II in the optimized mode but examples are in the debug configuration by default, they will not get compiled right away.

To compile the deal.II examples, you have to disable the debug mode. For this, edit the corresponding /var/mpishare/deal.II/examples/step-XX/Makefile, where XX stands for the example number you are currently trying. Look for the debug-mode = on line and change it to debug-mode = off.

Do not forget to disable the debug mode in the example's makefiles in order to be able to compile them.

To compile the program in the examples/step-1 folder of your deal.II source directory, type make to compile the software. You see that having a makefile is a great advantage. It will take about half a minute to compile the software, which will produce an executable of the same name as the parent directory.

To execute it, just type the following:

```
mpirun -n 1 ./step-1
```

 Please note that this program must only be executed on a single node, because it is not written for multiple processes.

You will see that this program produces two eps files that contain some graphical output. Let's now go into details of how the program works and what it does.

The program demonstrates how to create triangulation objects and how to loop over the geometric cells, namely the triangles. For this purpose, two grids are generated. One is a uniform square, and the other is a ring shape with a refinement towards the inner edge.

These give you an idea about the basis for every finite element software, which is a mesh generator that creates the mesh of the object that you want to do calculations on and a mesh iterator that handles very single geometric vertex, edge, or face of the mesh.

## Explaining the code

To go into more detail, let's have a look at the code lines. You will see that the code is very well documented. When you write software yourself, you should always add a lot of documentation and comment lines to your software. This will help others understand your software and also help you remember what you were thinking when you wrote it.

A very remarkable aspect of the deal.II library is its easy-to-use possibilities that output data to a file. Search for the grid_out.write_eps (triangulation, out) line, which outputs the triangulation object to a file in a .eps format. There are many other possible ways for outputting data.

The following figure shows you an example of two different grids that were written to .eps files:

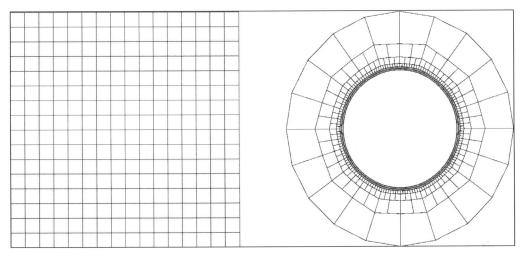

A uniform square grid (left) and radially refined circular shape (right)

You can open eps files with Adobe Photoshop.

# Dimensional independent code

A very nice feature of deal.II is that it provides the ability to program software independent of the number of space dimensions. This is possible because C++ supports a feature called **templates**. Independent means that you can write your code for 1D, 2D, or 3D applications at once without caring about special cases in your software.

To demonstrate this, you can compile example number 4 at the examples/step-4 location. Again, run it with ./step-4.

This will generate the following output:

```
Solving problem in 2 space dimensions.
   Number of active cells: 256
   Total number of cells: 341
   Number of degrees of freedom: 289
   26 CG iterations needed to obtain convergence.
Solving problem in 3 space dimensions.
   Number of active cells: 4096
   Total number of cells: 4681
   Number of degrees of freedom: 4913
   30 CG iterations needed to obtain convergence.
```

To understand the main advantage of the code, open the `main.cc` file and scroll down to the end. You will find the following code in the main function:

```
Step4<2> laplace_problem_2d;
laplace_problem_2d.run ();

Step4<3> laplace_problem_3d;
laplace_problem_3d.run ();
```

Notice that the first and the second pair of instructions use the same class named `Step4`. The edgy brackets behind the class name create instances of the predefined template with the corresponding number of dimensions. This provides a very flexible way to write general problem solvers for arbitrary dimensionalities.

# Iterative triangulation refinement

One more interesting thing is the possibility of deal.II automatically refining the mesh during the equation solving. Example 5 in the `step-5` directory (see the first example for the directory's location) calculates the solution of the Laplace-equation in 2D and 3D with nonhomogeneous Dirichlet boundary values. In this case, the equation $-\nabla a(x,y)\nabla u(x,y) = 1$ inside the circular area with u=0 on the border is solved. A practical application would be to solve the electric potential `u(x,y)` if a conductivity `a(x,y)` and a constant current density are given.

Or, `u(x,y)` can be the deflection of a membrane if `a(x,y)` is its stiffness.

The solution is calculated using the **conjugate gradients** (**CG**) method, which is an effective way to solve linear systems with symmetric, positive, and definite system matrices. You can refer to the following figure for more information. After each CG solution cycle, the number of the faces roughly doubles, leading to a more exact solution.

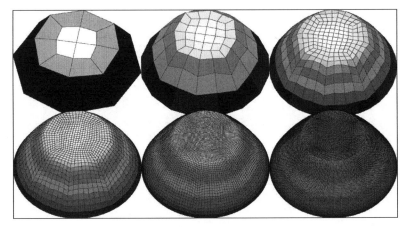

Dynamic grid refinement

# Parallel solution of elastic equations

Till now, all deal.II examples only used the first cluster node. They were thought to show you a few things that deal.II is able to do and how it can nicely output some graphics. In this example, however, you will see an example where a very computationally intense equation for the elastic deformation of a solid body is solved in parallel on a BeagleBone Black cluster using the deal.II library. Because deal.II supports an interface to the PETSc library, problems can be transferred to PETSc and solved on the cluster in parallel.

Let's first consider the mathematical starting point. The elastic equation is as follows:

$$-\partial_j\left(c_{ijkl}\partial_k u_l\right) = f_i$$

Here, c is the stiffness tensor, f is the force vector, and u is the resulting deformation vector. The implementation of such a linear equation system is very complicated. There are further explanations at `http://www.dealii.org/8.0.0/doxygen/deal.II/step_8.html` regarding the programming of deal.II to solve this.

While step-8 is still a serial solution of the problem, step-17 does the same using PETSc in parallel.

Go to the `examples/step-17` folder and compile the example program by typing the following:

```
make
```

Run it by typing the following:

```
mpirun -n 8 ./step-17
```

The output should be as follows:

```
Cycle 0:
    Number of active cells:       64
    Number of degrees of freedom: 162 (by partition:
16+25+18+22+18+23+18+22)
    Solver converged in 24 iterations.
Cycle 1:
    Number of active cells:       124
    Number of degrees of freedom: 302 (by partition:
44+31+37+37+37+37+35+44)
    Solver converged in 33 iterations.
    ...
Cycle 9:
    Number of active cells:       21472
    Number of degrees of freedom: 44002 (by partition: 5512+5483+5579+5427
+5490+5526+5447+5538)
    Solver converged in 265 iterations.
```

In the last step, the program solved an equation system with 44 thousand unknowns. In my example, it utilized 8 cluster nodes.

To view the calculated data, special software is required. You can use Visit, which is a data visualization software with a very broad spectrum of functionality. This will be described in the next subsection.

# The visualization of calculated data

Although deal.II can output data in various formats and you could always choose another format, if you cannot open special example files such as .gmv in the previous example, there is a highly sophisticated visualization software called Visit that is freely available on the Web.

You can download it to your computer from the following link in order to install and conveniently view the solution files from any remote location using the Samba network share, for example.

 Visit 2.7.3 will require around 520 MB of hard disk space during the installation.

After installing and starting Visit, you should get two windows: a kind of tool window on the left-hand side and a document window on the right-hand side.

There is a problem with the current .gmv importer and deal.II .gmv output files. In order to correctly load your simulation data, you should change example 17 to output .vtk files instead of .gmv files. For this, open the main.cc file and replace the following lines:

| Before | After |
|---|---|
| filename << "solution-" << cycle << ".gmv" | filename << "solution-" << cycle << ".vtk" |
| data_out.write_gmv | data_out.write_vtk |

Then, run step-17 again, as described previously.

On the left-hand side window, navigate to **File | Open...** in the **File** menu. The easiest way is to create a Windows network drive to connect to your mpishare.

In my case, this is `drive K`. In the **File open** dialog, you can then select this drive and access your deal.II output files as depicted in the following screenshot:

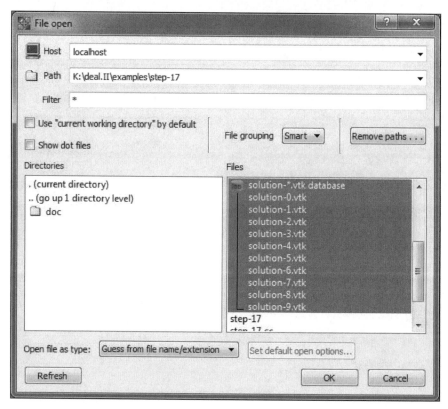

The Visit file's open dialog

As you can see, the generated `.vtk` files of the modified example 17 are automatically displayed as a database collection. Click on **OK** and don't be irritated if you see nothing. To see your data, you will have to select what you want to see next and add it to the plots list. For this, go to the left-hand side window and open the **Add** menu with the green plus sign. Go to **Pseudocolor** and select **x-displacement**.

This will load the x-component of the displacement solution vector into the plots list.

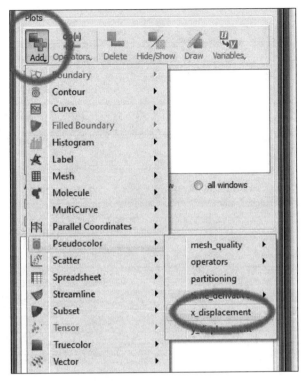

Add data to the plots list

Finally, with the added plot selected, click on the **Draw** button to visualize it:

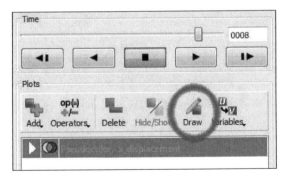

Draw a selected plot

You should now see the calculated data for the x-displacement of the solid body from simulation cycle 0.

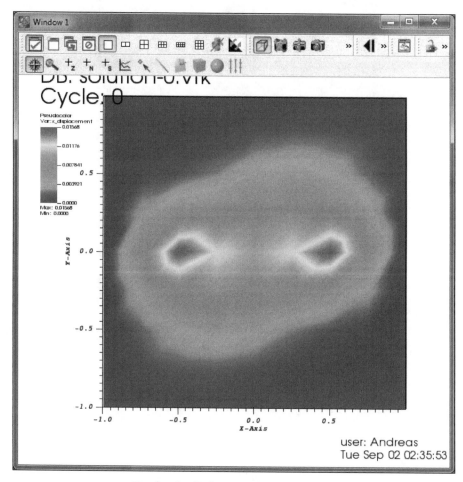

Simulated x-displacement data from cycle 0

As you can see, the grid is quite rough, and the solution could be much better. To view data from a later cycle, you can use the time slide in the left-hand side window, which actually picks one of our sequential cycles. Move the slider to the very right and you will get a display of the data from cycle 9.

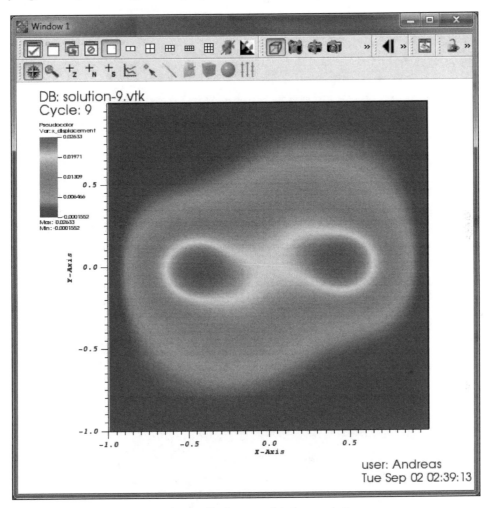

Simulated x-displacement data from cycle 9

Now, you can see that visualizing data with Visit is not very difficult. Also, complex output formats such as .vtk allow good data organization for complex simulations.

There is one very interesting feature that was saved along with our simulation data, namely the distribution of our mesh onto the different cluster nodes. To view this, click on the **Add** button in the left-hand side window, select **Pseudocolor**, and then select **partitioning**.

Click on **Draw** and you will see a map where each part depicts the portion of the solution calculated by a different cluster node.

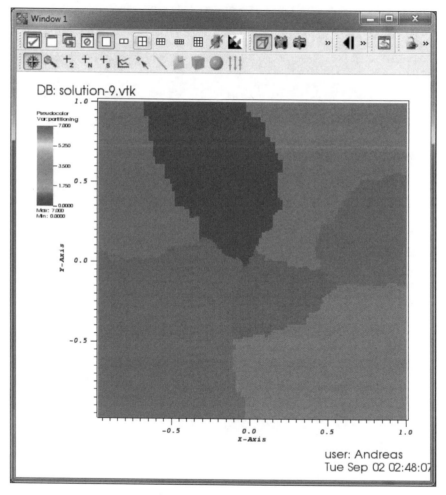

Node partitioning of the mesh grid

# Summary

In this last chapter, we saw some highly advanced applications of all our previously used packages together with the deal.II library. Of course, it was not possible to show you everything in detail; however, you were introduced to many techniques that are very important in order to write or understand modern simulation software for science, engineering, and many other areas.

You got to know about the deal.II library and how it is configured and built upon our previously compiled libraries PETSc and SLEPc. You were shown some important examples, which are part of the deal.II documentation, that demonstrate the power of your BeagleBone Black cluster. Mainly, these examples demonstrated triangulation to describe geometric objects and discussed the solution of Poisson's equation on one node in order to have a first look how deal.II works. We also discussed the parallel solution of elastic equations that calculate the deformation of a solid body in parallel and show how the full cluster can be used for scientific or engineering simulations.

If you do not understand everything and if you think it is too complicated to apply these techniques, don't be demotivated. The deal.II library is a very huge collection of code written by professional scientific researchers. There are many examples throughout the Internet, and it will take you some time and patience to get used to the style and rules. It is a good idea to start with the simplest examples and try to modify the code and play with it. This way, you will soon learn what is possible and what is not, and you will develop your own way of using libraries to perform high-end calculations on your self-built BeagleBone cluster.

# References

The operating system used with the BeagleBone Black boards is `Ubuntu Linux for ARM`:

- For all downloads of BeagleBone Black, visit `http://www.armhf.com/download/`
- To download BeagleBone for Ubuntu Precise 12.04.4 LTS, visit `http://www.armhf.com/boards/beaglebone-black/#precise`

The following links provide access to the third-party software used in this book, which is not part of the used Linux distribution:

- To download Putty SSH Client, visit `http://www.putty.org`
- To download the Network shared storage, visit `www.samba.org`
- To download the Windows secure copy protocol software, visit `http://winscp.net/eng/download.php`
- To download ScaLAPACK, visit `http://www.netlib.org/scalapack/#_scalapack_version_2_0_2`
- To download the ScaLAPACK installer, visit `http://www.netlib.org/scalapack/scalapack_installer.tgz`
- To download the ScaLAPACK `pdpttr` example, visit `http://acts.nersc.gov/scalapack/hands-on/etc/pdpttr_2/pdpttr_2.c.html`
- To download PETSc, visit `http://ftp.mcs.anl.gov/pub/petsc/release-snapshots/petsc-3.4.1.tar.gz`
- To download the PETSc user manual, visit `http://www.mcs.anl.gov/petsc/petsc-current/docs/manual.pdf`

- To download PETSc's linear solver examples, visit `http://www.mcs.anl.gov/petsc/petsc-current/src/ksp/ksp/examples/tutorials/index.html`

- To download PETSc SNES example 5, visit `www.mcs.anl.gov/petsc/petsc-3.4/src/snes/examples/tutorials/ex5.c.html`

- To download SLEPc, visit `http://www.grycap.upv.es/slepc/download/download.htm`

- To download SLEPc's handy examples, visit `http://www.grycap.upv.es/slepc/handson/`

- To download deal.II, visit `https://dealii.googlecode.com/files/deal.II-7.3.0.tar.gz`

- To download deal.II example 8, visit `http://www.dealii.org/8.0.0/doxygen/deal.II/step_8.html`

- To download Visit, go to `https://wci.llnl.gov/simulation/computer-codes/visit/executables`

# Index

Delaunay criterion  110
direct solvers
    versus iterative solvers  98
distributed memory systems  59
domain name server (DNS)  64
dynamic linking  21

# E

elastic equations
    solution  123, 124
Ethernet multiport switch  33
example, deal.II
    code  120
    compiling  119
    dimensional independent code  121, 122
    download link  134
    elastic equations, solving  123, 124
    iterative triangulation refinement  122
example, PETSc
    compiling  89
    direct solvers, versus iterative solvers  98
    download link  134
    executing  89
    linear equations, solving with
        SuperLU_DIST  92-97
    nonlinear equations, solving with
        SNES  99-101
    simple vector math  89-92
example, SLEPc
    cluster's scaling ability,
        demonstrating  105, 106
    compiling  104
    download link  134
Executable and Linking Format (ELF)  21
external network storage  46-48

# F

file transfer, BeagleBone master node
    about  55
    FTP server, used  55
    WinSCP used  56, 57
file transfer protocol (FTP)  55

finite elements
    about  109, 111
    example  111-113
Fortran library  75
FTP server
    about  55
    used, for file transfer  55

# G

Generalized Minimal Residual
    (GMRES)  83
general-purpose I/O (GPIO)  11
gid parameter  48
Grand Unified Bootloader (GRUB)  39
graphical libraries, PETSc
    installing  84

# H

hardware, BeagleBone Black
    central processing unit  10, 11
    control buttons  11-13
    I/O interfaces  11-13
    onboard memory and flash storage  13
high-level programming  19
hub  31

# I

installation image, master node
    creating  38
    image size, adapting to card space  42
    writing, to microSD card  40, 41
installation, PETSc
    on cluster nodes  88
installation process, Ubuntu
    steps  40, 41
iterative solvers
    versus direct solvers  98

# K

Krylov subspace  83

## L

**library files, ScaLAPACK**
librefblas.a 74
libreflapack.a 74
libscalapack.a 74
libtmg.a 74
**Linear Algebra Package (LAPACK) 71**
**linear equations**
solving, with SuperLU_DIST 92-98
**linear solvers**
BiConjugate Gradient Stabilized
(BiCGSTAB) 83
Conjugate Gradients (CG) 83
Conjugate Gradients Squared (CGS) 83
Generalized Minimal Residual (GMRES) 83
Transpose-Free Quasi-Minimal
Residual (TFQMR) 83
**Line Search 84**
**Linux host environment 38**
**low-cost power source**
ATX power supply, modifying 29, 30
power cables 29
power requirements 29
using 28
**low-level programming 19**

## M

**makefiles**
about 118
using 119
**master boot record (MBR) 39**
**Message Passing Interface.** *See* **MPI**
**Metis 87**
**MPI**
about 59, 60
development 60
features 60
process control 61
software structure 62
**MPI_Barrier function 68**

**mpic++ 65**
**mpiexec command 70**
**MPI_Finalize command 67**
**mpirun command 66**

## N

**network backbone**
setting up 31
**Network shared storage**
download link 133
**network topology**
about 31, 32
Ethernet multiport switch 33
RJ45 network cables 33
**nibble 18**
**nonlinear equations**
solving, with SNES 99-101
**nonlinear solvers**
Line Search 84
Trusted Region 84

## O

**OpenMPI**
about 63
configuring 63
default hostfile, configuring 64
downloading 63
installing 63
linear mathematical problems 71
packages 63
ScaLAPACK, using 72
simple node synchronization 68
test application, creating 65-68
value, passing between nodes 69, 70
**operating system installation,**
**on master node**
internal eMMC, flashing 45, 46
network interface, configuring 44, 45
performing 43
**operating systems**
about 16
ARMhf images 16
Ubuntu 12.04 ARMhf Linux system 17

## Thank you for buying
# Building a BeagleBone Black Super Cluster

## About Packt Publishing

Packt, pronounced 'packed', published its first book "*Mastering phpMyAdmin for Effective MySQL Management*" in April 2004 and subsequently continued to specialize in publishing highly focused books on specific technologies and solutions.

Our books and publications share the experiences of your fellow IT professionals in adapting and customizing today's systems, applications, and frameworks. Our solution based books give you the knowledge and power to customize the software and technologies you're using to get the job done. Packt books are more specific and less general than the IT books you have seen in the past. Our unique business model allows us to bring you more focused information, giving you more of what you need to know, and less of what you don't.

Packt is a modern, yet unique publishing company, which focuses on producing quality, cutting-edge books for communities of developers, administrators, and newbies alike. For more information, please visit our website: www.packtpub.com.

## About Packt Open Source

In 2010, Packt launched two new brands, Packt Open Source and Packt Enterprise, in order to continue its focus on specialization. This book is part of the Packt Open Source brand, home to books published on software built around Open Source licenses, and offering information to anybody from advanced developers to budding web designers. The Open Source brand also runs Packt's Open Source Royalty Scheme, by which Packt gives a royalty to each Open Source project about whose software a book is sold.

## Writing for Packt

We welcome all inquiries from people who are interested in authoring. Book proposals should be sent to author@packtpub.com. If your book idea is still at an early stage and you would like to discuss it first before writing a formal book proposal, contact us; one of our commissioning editors will get in touch with you.

We're not just looking for published authors; if you have strong technical skills but no writing experience, our experienced editors can help you develop a writing career, or simply get some additional reward for your expertise.

## BeagleBone Robotic Projects

ISBN: 978-1-78355-932-9          Paperback: 244 pages

Create complex and exciting robotic projects with the BeagleBone Black

1. Get to grips with robotic systems.

2. Communicate with your robot and teach it to detect and respond to its environment.

3. Develop walking, rolling, swimming, and flying robots.

## Building a Home Security System with BeagleBone

ISBN: 978-1-78355-960-2          Paperback: 120 pages

Build your own high-tech alarm system at a fraction of the cost

1. Build your own state-of-the-art security system.

2. Monitor your system from anywhere you can receive e-mail.

3. Add control of other systems such as sprinklers and gates.

4. Save thousands on monitoring and rental fees.

Please check **www.PacktPub.com** for information on our titles

## BeagleBone Home Automation

ISBN: 978-1-78328-573-0       Paperback: 178 pages

Live your sophisticated dream with home automation using BeagleBone

1. Practical approach to home automation using BeagleBone; starting from the very basics of GPIO control and progressing up to building a complete home automation solution.

2. Covers the operating principles of a range of useful environment sensors, including their programming and integration to the server application.

## Rapid BeagleBoard Prototyping with MATLAB and Simulink

ISBN: 978-1-84969-604-3       Paperback: 152 pages

Leverage the power of BeagleBoard to develop and deploy practical embedded projects

1. Develop and validate your own embedded audio/video applications rapidly with Beagleboard.

2. Create embedded Linux applications on a pure Windows PC.

3. Full of illustrations, diagrams, and tips for rapid Beagleboard prototyping with clear, step-by-step instructions and hands-on examples.

Please check **www.PacktPub.com** for information on our titles